THE

RAPTURE OF THE CHURCH

AND

THE EVENTS OF THE END TIME

By

Adeyinka Adebisi Lawani

DEDICATION

This book is dedicated to the Lord Jesus Christ who is my Lord and my personal savior. He died for my sake so that I can have eternal life and now I have eternal life. I give you oh God all the glory; honor and adoration.

I also dedicate it to my loving wife Oluwakemi Olushola Lawani, a very wonderful woman of God who operates in the Prophetic office; she has been an inspiration to me especially in encouraging me to put this piece together. To all my children: Oluwashemiloore, Ayobami, Inioluwa and Toluwalashe.

Dedicated also to my spiritual family, all the members and ministers of our Church, The Beauty of Christ Church. God bless you all.

TABLE OF CONTENTS

ACKNOWLEDGMENTS

I want to appreciate the Almighty God for the good health and wisdom that He has given to me to write this book. This book should have been out many years ago, but somehow I was unable to put it together because I could not put the thoughts together.

During the covid-19 lock down, after much prayers and encouragement from my wife Oluwakemi Olushola Lawani, I received the inspiration to forge ahead. I honestly appreciate that encouragement from my wife. She has been very supportive. God bless you sweetheart.

Special mention must be made of Brother Etenabe Clement Taiwo who was one of the workers under me in The Redeemed Christian Church of God, where I was a pastor, he wrote the foreword to this book. He is a man that is so versed in the scriptures; in fact he is a mighty man in the scripture. I learnt so much from him although I was his pastor. He is really endowed with knowledge especially in the area of eschatology. God bless you sir.

I also appreciate the role played by Dr Babatunde Omidiji of the department of Mechanical Engineering Obafemi Awolowo University Ile-Ife.

He is one of the editors of this book. He diligently went through this book to ensure that it is error free.

I also appreciate Mr. Adeleye my in-law, who is very instrumental to the publishing of this book, the Lord bless you in Jesus mighty name.

ADEYINKA ADEBISILAWANI

+2348057076600, +2347069695369

adelawani71@gmail.com

FOREWORD

The study and doctrines of the end of all things is called Eschatology. The issue of Rapture, the emergency of the Antichrist and the great tribulation has become a serious controversy over the years among Bible scholars.

Reasons being the fact that scholars with different schools of thought have misplaced the event of the Rapture.

Although some schools of thought were able to prove and support their claims with scriptures. Nevertheless, they are not to be condemned or crucified.

The Pre-Tribulation, Mid-Tribulation, Post tribulation and Pre-Wrath Rapture of the church are all in the schools of thought that the Rapture can take place in one of these.

I am going to limit the scope of this study to The Pre-Tribulation event that is the school of thought that the Rapture will take place before the greattribulation.

This is what majority of Christians believe from onset before a little distraction from the original.

In this book, a detail of Rapture is fully explained as far as Pre-Tribulation Rapture is concerned. It is an exciting deep expository book which answers many unanswered questions.

The events before the Rapture, the Rapture and events that will be thereafter.

The rise of the Antichrist who is called son of perdition, his agreement with Israel and his reign of terror which will lead to the great tribulation also referred to as the time of Jacob's trouble. The details of God's wrath are all discussed in full.

The two mysterious witnesses are also discussed and their mission in the end time.

Now Christ's return will Mark the end of the Antichrist's rule and all that is called corruption and unrighteousness.

The beginning of a new era of 1000 years reign of Christ called The Millennium. The mystery of the short rule of Satan is exposed.

Christ will rule the world with His holy saints.

What shall be after all these?

What will happen to people who remain after Rapture?

Will all flesh die before the millennium and after?

Will people give birth to young ones after and during the millennium?

When will the world be finally destroyed?

Are we going to live in heaven forever?

And what will happen to all the saints thereafter?

These are the question people ask. All these are dealt with in this book. Join me as we go on a trip to unfold the future event that is to come which is gradually unfolding. The Rapture of the believers!

The Rapture the (Believers) Church is the hope of the Christians

If we don't have the knowledge of the end, how will we be able to stand in the time of adversity? It is going to be a time when one's faith will be proved, a time when Christians whom one would have thought strong will fall and many will be greatly disappointed and offended, many will backslide. It will remain only you and you alone, then salvation will come amidst all these.

Only those who read and are wise will survive

Now is the time when people are scared and the heart of men begins to melt and fail them because of the fear of the unknown.

It is the time to focus on heavenly things while still doing business without defrauding one another, it is the time to return to God and retrace one's footsteps back from sins and errors, only true repentance can bring mercy. Those who know their God and walk in understanding with Him will escape through the Rapture.

The Antichrist must come as ordained and programmed by God, Satan will be allowed to fully rule this Earth in lawlessness and iniquity called Mystery at least for a short period in the last seven years of this age. But those days must be shortened if any flesh is to be saved during the tribulation.

It must occur, it must happen; only the church and God can delay it. The church cannot stop nor prevent it; it is already in the program of God. Rapture of the church will bring about a full blown manifestation of the Antichrist!

- **Etenabe Clement Taiwo**

CHAPTER ONE

THE PRE RAPTURE EVENTS

*And When These Things Begin To
Come To Pass, Then Look Up, And
Lift Up Your Heads; For Your
Redemption Draweth Nigh*

LUKE 21:28

THE PRE RAPTURE EVENTS

When the Lord Jesus Christ was leaving the earth, He gave assurances to His disciples that He will surely be coming back. He told them in the book of John chapter 14, that He was going to prepare a place for them, so that where He will be, they would also be there. He made 2 statements that sounded like a contradiction, but there is no contradiction in the word of God.

He said, He would come like a thief in the night.

Mathew 24:42-44says

42: Watch therefore: for you know not what hour your Lord doth come.

43: But know this that if the good man of the house had known in what watch the thief would come, he would have watched, and would not have suffered his house to be broken up

44: Therefore be ye also ready: for in such an hour as ye think not the Son of man cometh.

The statement above is also corroborated by the two leading apostles: Peter and Paul.

In 2 Peter 3:10, Bible says

> **10: But the day of the Lord will come as a thief in the night; in the which the heavens shall pass away with a great noise and the elements shall melt with fervent heat, the earth also and the works that are therein shall be burned up.**

Apostle Paul also made a similar statement in
I Thessalonians 5:2

> **5:2 "for yourselves know perfectly that the day of the Lord so cometh as a thief in the night"**

The implication of the above statements is that nobody knows the hour that the Lord shall come. While Jesus was in the flesh, He confirmed to His disciples that even Himself does not know the exact hour, neither the angels in Heaven. But it is important to note that the glorified Jesus knows. Jesus Christ is God, so He knows all things.

The other statement made by our Lord is found in Revelation 1:7. It says

> **7: Behold, He cometh with clouds and every eye shall see Him, and they also which pierced Him: And all kindred of the earth shall wail because of Him. Even so Amen!**

Also **Acts 1:9-11**. Looking at both statements clearly, It sounds contradictory, but since it is known that there is no controversy in the word, it can be concluded that the statements are both referring to His coming which will be in two phases:

(A)   The Raptures of the Church (I Thessalonians5:2)
(B)   His second physical coming-Parousia (Acts 1:9-11)

The Bible speaks about several events that will take place before the Rapture. There shall be wars and rumors of wars, pestilence, famine, diseases without cure. All these events shall make the hearts of unbelievers to melt with fear. Today as this book is being written, Syria is engaged in a bloody civil war, Somalia is also engaged in war, a confrontation between America and Iran has just been doused. Kingdoms are threatening other kingdoms. North Korea is threatening every other country that are voicing out against its atrocities.

In the year 2019, a pandemic (Covid -19) broke out that is affecting the whole world. The pandemic is already shutting down global economies, leading to hunger, racism, starvation and frustration with so many job losses and many people are already committing suicide.

If the Christians do not unite in Prayers and action, it may eventually lead to one world government, with commerce being controlled from the Centre, one single currency etc.

All these will be discussed in details in another chapter. The calamity that can occur from these entire events before the Rapture is that people's rights can be withdrawn or abused. There has never been a time in recent history where Churches are closed globally, businesses shut down and people are forcefully quarantined in their homes like now.

Bill gates who is not a Doctor (but with considerable investment in the health sector) is vigorously pushing for vaccines under his ID2020 Alliance program. The vaccine will come with chips which will make it easy to identify and track those who have not been vaccinated.

He is already calling on government to isolate people who refuse the Vaccine as they will be endangering other people who are vaccinated; he also subtly said that large crowds may not be able to gather together until around year 2030 when a substantial number of people would have been vaccinated. All these are targeted against the Church so that the church cannot fellowship together again.

Our fellowship has a way of creating positive vibration that affects the world demonic system.

In the book of Revelation from chapter 1 – 3, Jesus wrote a letter to the seven Churches in Asia, the churches are:
1. Ephesus
2. Smyrna

3. Pergamos
4. Thyatira
5. Sardis
6. Philadelphia
7. Laodicea

The essence of the letter is to tell each of the Churches to prepare for the Rapture. He indicated their good works and also mandated them to repent where necessary.

1. Ephesus: The Ephesian church was given 10 commendations, one condemnation and they were commanded to repent and return to their first love.

2. Smyrna: They were commended for 3 things. No condemnation.

3. Pergamos: The Church received 3 commendations and four condemnations. Christ admonished them to repent.

4. Thyatira: Christ had six commendations for them and 4 condemnations. They were admonished torepent.

5. Sardis: It was a Church that had a fake reputation. They have a reputation of being alive but they are actually dead. Their works was not found acceptable before God. They were admonished to repent.

6. Philadelphia: The Church was given four commendations by God and no condemnation.

7. Laodicea: The Church represented the most canal of the seven Churches, it was a lukewarm Church that Christ was ready to spew out of His mouth. It was a completely dead Church, careless, indifferent with no zeal. Christ admonished the church to repent.

Today's Church is very similar to the Church of Sardis and Laodicea. It is not preparing for the coming of the Lord again; it is into big time worldliness. Most Churches hardly teach about righteousness, Holiness and the Rapture, but it has concentrated itself on only the teachings of prosperity (which is not bad in itself). To make the church prepared, its teaching must be balanced, not lopsided or tilted towards only prosperity.

In some Churches today, riches are equated to holiness. They believe that if you are not rich you are definitely not a child of God. So if you are not rich, you cannot hold position or even become a pastor in such Churches. No wonder, worldliness has really entered into the church.

The Church must repent so that it can be Raptured.
The world is not the home of the believer, a day is coming very soon when the trumpet shall be blown and the righteous shall go to meet with the Lord in the air. Every believer should be looking forward to that day.

All the structures that the Anti-Christ will use to govern the world are being put in place. The time is very short. Below are some of the recent global developments

CURRENCY

The world is discussing about a single digital currency already. They have been selling the ideas to people all over the world about the need to cancel paper currency because it is capable of spreading diseases and other flimsy excuses so that their agenda can be carried out.
As at today, there are over one thousand digital currencies or crypto currencies already in existence. Example are Bitcoin, Bitcoin cash, Dogecoin, Ven, Ethereum, Litecoin etc these can be transacted within seconds without third parties. The world will eventually unite on which currency to adopt under a single world government under the Anti-Christ.

UN SEEDPROGRAM

The United Nations seed program is already in place.
The idea is to collect all known seeds and alter them genetically (GMO). So that nobody can even plant without buying the seeds from them and remember if you are left behind you can't even buy without the mark of the beast or the number of his name.

The genetically modified seeds are such that if it is planted in the first year, there will be a very bountiful harvest. Once the seeds from the previous harvest are planted, it will not germinate, so even seeds for every planting season must be obtained or purchased from the center. To be able to do these purchases, the person doing the purchasing must receive the mark of the Anti-Christ or the number of his name failure of which he or she will not be able to do thetransaction.

WORLD SINGLE RELIGION

The world is collaborating already about the formation of a single world religion under the guise of peace. These efforts are largely being promoted by big wigs especially the pope. The religion will be ecumenical in nature.

GAY MOVEMENT

The gay movement is also part of the end time agenda. The world suffered a major setback under the Obama administration in this area. He legalized all manner of unacceptable practices especially the LGBTQ community thereby making ungodly things look normal. In the western world, homosexuality has become normal.

The Anti-Christ himself will manifest as a homosexual.

Daniel 11:36-37 says:

36. And the king shall do according to his will; and he shall exalt himself, and magnify himself above any god, and shall speak marvelous thing against the God of gods, and shall prosper till the indignation be accomplished: for that is determined shall be done.

37. **Neither shall he regard the God of his fathers <u>nor the desire of women,</u> nor regard any god: for he shall magnify himself above all.**

TECHNOLOGY

Perhaps the greatest tool that will be at the disposal of the Anti-Christ will be technology. Over the years, technology has developed at such an alarming rate. From the time Electricity (this is probably the greatest invention) was discovered, every other invention seems to just fall into place. Most other inventions are hinged in one way or the other on Electricity.

Man invented automobile, aero plane, computer etc. Flying which was once thought to be impossible has been achieved, this is being improved upon on a daily basis with some of them speeding faster than the speed of sound in the air(supersonic).

Man invented the television which at a time is only required to play recorded messages, but now carries life telecasts.

The 70s, 80s and 90s witnessed a tremendous improvement in the telephone industry. From cable telephony to wireless technology, man has conquered his environment, travelled to the moon and also planning to travel to Mars. The invention of computers in the 20th century became a game changer. Data were being processed at a very high speed, information storage and access become easier, the face of business changed. The world had to change to face the realities; the world moved from the jet age to the internet age and now the age of The Internet of Things (IOT), with the change came fraud etc. Credit and Debit cards were linked to bank accounts through the use of a chip on the card.

The mobile phone today has combined almost all technologies together to become the most powerful tool of the present and also the future. it is a television, a phone, a camera, a live transmission equipment, a business tool, a bank, a doctor, a compass and just everything.

The world in under ten years has moved from second generation (2G) to the fifth generation (5G) spectrum, under 3G and 4G, you can do video call which was completely unimaginable years back.

God has been using technology to speak to scientists. When Christians in one location pray for other Christians in other locations, the unbeliever will be laughing trying to imagine how the prayer will get to the location.

But believers know that there is no distance in the realm of the Spirit. Now even the distance in the realm of the physical has been reduced. You can now do a live chat or video call which was impossible just some few years back.

As this book is being written, there is an outbreak of Corona Virus (Covid-19), 5G is also massively deployed despite all the global outcries. No independent studies have been conducted on the health implications of the 5G. Conspiracy theorists believe that it is the radiation from 5G that is responsible for the massive deaths although there is an outbreak of Covid-19, they believe that Covid-19 is being used as a cover up so that the telecoms cannot be sued for the massive deaths. Until an independent study is conducted, this can neither be denied nor affirmed.

5G has a lot to offer in terms of speed, human/machine interaction. But the ultimate as I believe is to take over the human mind for easy manipulation, so that whatever comes into the human mind, can be transcribed.

It is also believed in some quarters that the 5G will also take away the human liberty/freedom as it will be easy to monitor what everybody is doing per time especially when linked to a chip in a human body. This will be very resourceful for the Anti- Christ, may be at the time of his manifestation, the world will be on 8G or 9G or even 10G or whatever. It will be a very important tool for the Anti-Christ to communicate with people who have been chipped. The communication can be done online real time.

VACCINATION PROGRAM

The world vaccination program is being promoted by the tech giant Bill Gates in association with ID 2020 Alliance under the guise of providing vaccination to prevent viral diseases. The "Philanthropist" is pushing for a vaccine that is chip enabled. Ordinarily, this is a good idea since prevention is better and cheaper than cure. The challenge is that the vaccine will come with a chip and the chip in the vaccine will carry all the information of the recipient and he is "encouraging" the whole world to go for the vaccine.

Once vaccinated, the recipient can travel to anywhere in the world without posing as a health risk to others, such a person will be given an ID which is connected to the chip in the body and that can be verified through a computer.

The project should be suspicious for any discerning mind. Despite the outstanding breakthrough of using chloroquine for the treatment of Covid-19, the use of chloroquine is being discouraged by the proponents of the vaccines. It is believed in some quarters that the chip may subject the recipient to mind control. It is also believed among the Christian community that these are just early trials of the Mark of the beast which will manifest under the Anti-Christ. This is being gradually introduced so that when it is formally released, the world system will already be accustomed to it.

Remember, Bible says that the mark will be on the right hand or on the fore head. Time will eventually expose the true purpose of the vaccine.

The vaccine has come under increased attack from most countries of the world and especially the US where the Supreme Court has ruled against forceful vaccination.

CHAPTER TWO

THE RAPTURE

Then We Which Are Alive And Remain Shall Be Caught Up Together With Them In The Clouds, To Meet The Lord In The Air; And So Shall We Ever Be With The Lord

1 Thessalonians 4:17

THE RAPTURE

The word RAPTURE is not in the Bible, but it is used to describe a Spiritual experience. Rapture is defined as the sudden catching up of the saints and the dead in Christ to be with the lord in the air or the sudden disappearance of the saints.

There are about 6 types of Rapture in the Bible, but the fourth one which we are expecting now will be the greatest and most memorable of them all. The experience was described by Apostle Paul in 1 Thessalonians 4: 15-17 which says:

15: For this we say unto you by the word of the lord, that we which are alive and remain unto the coming of the lord shall not prevent them which are asleep.

16: For the lord himself shall descend from heaven with a shout with the voice of an angel, and with the trump of God and the dead In Christ shall rise first

17: Then we which are alive and remain shall be caught up together with them in the clouds and so shall we ever be with the lord.

The above is the description of the Rapture. May we all be partakers in the mighty name of Jesus. It is an event which

God has prepared for prepared souls. It will happen so suddenly that it will take the world by surprise.

The day will cause a lot of devastation, horror and confusion. This will make the world to quickly form a government of unity to take care of the problems that will arise as a result of the event. Structures are already in place that will make such a decision easy to achieve.

The Rapture of the church will still be discussed in details in this same chapter. In the book of Revelation the event is immediately after chapter 3.

Chapters 1-3 of Revelation represent the things of the church. It is important to note that Revelation chapters 4-18 does not in any way concern the Church, it concerns only the Jews and the careless Christians that will miss the Rapture.

The great tribulation is referred to as the time of Jacob's trouble (Jeremiah 30:7). The great tribulation as will be discussed later pertains to only the brothers of our Lord Jesus Christ in the flesh. However, anyone that misses the Rapture and is associated with Christ will come under severe judgment from the Anti- Christ whose mission is to opposeChrist.

OTHER TYPES OF RAPTURE IN THE SCRIPTURE

Enoch: This is the first man to be Raptured. He walked with God and God took him. There is no account in the scripture of his death. Genesis 5:22-24 says

> **22: And Enoch walked with God after he begat Methuselah three hundred years and begat sons and daughters**
>
> **23: and all the days of Enoch were three hundred and sixty five years**
>
> **24: And Enoch walked with God and he was not; for God took him.**

He just disappeared all of a sudden. Another very vivid description of him is in Hebrews 11:5 which says

> **25: By faith Enoch was translated that he should not see death and he was not found because God has translated him for before his translation he had this testimony that he pleased God.**

And God took him away suddenly and he is with God in heaven in the flesh. The Hebrew passage gave additional information by using the word "Translated". This is a confirmation that Enoch did not die but was Raptured or translated into heaven.

Elijah: Elijah is the second man to experience Rapture in the scripture. Elijah ended his personal ministry prematurely by asking God to choose a successor since he became tired of his calling. Unfortunately he is the only person in the scripture who appointed a successor while alive. It is important to note that Elijah still have a role to perform in the end time just like Enoch. Bible says in II kings 2:11

11: And it came to pass as they still went on and talked that behold there appeared a chariot of fire and horses of fire and parted them both asunder and Elijah went up by a whirl wind into heaven.

He is also with God in his natural body and he was taken suddenly that he should not see death but for an appointed time. He was Raptured.

Jesus Christ: Jesus Christ is the savior of the world. He died for the sin of mankind, resurrected on the third day for the justification of the world. He is the first to enter immortality. After three and half year of his ministry, He was put to death, He became alive in the spirit, went to hell and forcefully collected from the devil, the keys of death and hell. In Revelation 1:18 Bible says

18: I am he that liveth and was dead and behold I am alive forever more amen and have the key of hell and of death.

Read Hebrew 2:14 for proper understanding. After completing His assignment, He gathered His disciples and was Raptured in their presence.

Acts 1:9-11 *says:*

9: And when He had spoken these things, while they beheld, He was taken up: and a cloud received Him out of their sight"

10: And while they looked steadfastly toward heaven as He went up behold, two men stood by them in white apparel.

11: which also said, ye men of Galilee, why stand ye gazing up into heaven? This same Jesus, which is taken up from you, shall so come in like manner as ye have seen him go into heaven.

Jesus Christ is the first fruit from the dead and the first to enter into immortality; He was Raptured after His assignment.

WHEN WILL THE CHURCH BE RAPTURED?

The timing of the Rapture of the Church has become a controversial subject. There are three (3) Schools of thought on the subject, namely:

1. THE PRE TRIBULATION CHRISTIANS
2. THE MID TRIBULATION CHRISTIANS
3. THE POST TRIBULATION CHRISTIANS

1. THE PRE TRIBULATION CHRISTIANS:

We believe that the Church will be taken away ahead of the Great Tribulation. We believe that the Church was born in tribulation and it is still experiencing varying degrees of tribulations. In fact Jesus Christ promised the church tribulation and persecution.

Bible says in John 16:33

33: These things I have spoken unto you, that in me ye might have peace. In the world ye shall have tribulation: but be ye of good cheer; I have overcome the world.

Romans 8:35 says

35: Who shall separate us from the love of Christ? Shall tribulation or distress, or persecution, or famine or nakedness or peril, or sword?

Another very interesting passage in scripture is found in Mark 10:29-30

29: And Jesus answered and said verily I say unto you, there is no man that hath left house, or brethren, or sisters, or father, or mother, or wife, or children, or lands for my sake and the gospel's.

30: But he shall receive an hundred fold now in this time, houses and brethren, and sisters, and mothers and children, and lands with *PERSECUTIONS;* and in the world to come eternal life.

No genuine Christian will ever deny his Lord and master because of affliction resulting from persecution. The Church is already suffering tribulations and persecutions, as a matter of fact if we are not persecuted as Christians then there is something we are not doing right. But we must understand that God Has not appointed us unto wrath (1 Thessalonians 5:9). The Church of God will not be around during the Great tribulation.

Apostle Paul confirmed it in II Thessalonians 2:3- 8 that we will escape the Great tribulation. It is very emphatic.

3: Let no man deceive you by any means; for that day shall not come, except there comes a falling away first and that man of sin be revealed, the son of perdition;

4: Who opposeth and exalteth himself above all that is called God or that is worshiped so that he as God sitteth in the temple of God, shewing himself that he is God

5: Remember ye not, that, when I was yet with you I told you these things?

6: And now ye know what witholdeth that he might be revealed in his time.

7: For the mystery of iniquity doth already work; only he who now letteth will let, until he be taken out of the way
8: And then shall that wicked be revealed, whom the lord shall consume with the spirit of his mouth, and shall destroy with the brightness of His coming:

In some quarters it is believed that he that letteth is the Holy Spirit but that assertion is not true because the Holy Spirit is God and cannot be taken out of the way. That sounds like heresy. He that Letteth is the Church and until it is taken out of the way (Raptured), before the Anti-Christ can be manifested. Compare verse 3 and verse 7. Before the Anti-Christ can manifest, the Church will be taken away. Glory to God.

The Great tribulation happening after the Rapture makes understanding the timing easier. Anybody that remains knowing that something remarkable has taken place in the world will know that they have to start counting 7 years after the event. A further proof that the Rapture will take place before the Great tribulation is found in Daniel 9:20-27:

24: seventy weeks are determined upon thy people (Jews) and upon the holy city

(Jerusalem), to finish the transgression and to make an end of sins and to make reconciliation for iniquity and to bring in Everlasting righteousness and to seal up the vision and prophecy and to anoint the most holy.

(Kindly note that the emphasis is mine).

Here in Daniel chapter nine, it is the Jews and Jerusalem that is the subject, not the Church because the Church would been Raptured.

2.   THE MID TRIBULATION CHRISTIANS:

The mid tribulation Christians believe that the Rapture will take place in the first three and half years of the Great tribulation. They believe that they will see the manifestation of the Anti-Christ and also experience the lesser tribulation period. However, once the Anti-Christ begins the persecution, they will be Raptured and will not experience the horrible part of the Great tribulation.

The question to the mid tribulation Christian is how will they know that the Great tribulation has started?

Many people in history were thought to be the Anti-Christ, example Benito Mussolini, Adolf Hitler, Alexander the Great and Napoleon Bonaparte etc. It turned out that they were not. Going by the above argument if any of the above persons were to be the Anti Christ, the Church should have been Raptured 3 ½ years into their reign of terror.

3. POST TRIBULATIONCHRISTIANS:

The post tribulation Christians believe that the pre tribulation and mid tribulation Christians are very lazy Christians who are looking for an easy way out and are not ready to face the Great tribulation. They have a lot of good arguments that looks scriptural. They draw their conclusions and references from the teachings of our Lord Jesus Christ in Matthew 24:1-END (please read) which has nothing to do with the Rapture but the parousia.

A very close look at Matthew 24, there our Lord Jesus Christ was talking about 2 distinct events all directed at the Jews (the elect). Salvation is by the Jews and for the Jews. The Jews rejected Jesus and we the Gentiles were grafted in. Matthew 24:34says

34: verily I say unto you, this generation shall not pass, till all these things be fulfilled.

Well that generation has passed and the Rapture has not taken place. The first part of the prophecy has been fulfilled which has to do with the destruction of Jerusalem and the temple. That was fulfilled in 70 AD by the Roman army led by future emperor Titus with Tiberius Julius Alexander as his second-in- command. They besieged Jerusalem and conquered it in the same year and destroyed the temple. No stone was left on another.

It was fulfilled in that generation.

The other part of the prophecy used by the post tribulation Christians is Matthew 24:20-22, 29-31

20: **But pray that your flight be not in the winter, neither on the Sabbath day.**

21: for then shall be Great tribulation, such as was not since the beginning of the world to this time, no nor ever shall be.

22: And except those days should be shortened, there shall no flesh be saved: but for the elect sake those days shall be shortened.

They argue that the elect are the Christians who will definitely be there during the Great tribulation. However, if you look at the verse 20, you will understand that Jesus was talking to the Jewish community. You can start reading from Matthew 23 for clarity. In Matthew 24:20

20: But pray…neither on the Sabbath.

The Jews by law are not permitted to travel more than one mile on the Sabbath (Acts 1:12) and the orthodox Jews still observe that law. If they are attacked on the Sabbath day, they will run one mile and stop; they will then be overrun by their enemies. This law does **not** apply to Christians as we do not keep the Sabbath.

Verse 22 also talks about the elects. Who are the elects? The Jews are the elect of God but since they rejected salvation, we the Christian Gentiles became the elect by Grace.

Verse 29-31 speaks about the redemption of the Jews after the Great tribulation. Verse 31 speaks about their gathering to Jerusalem immediately after the Great Tribulation from the four quarters of heaven that is from the North, South, West and East into Jerusalem thereby fulfilling prophecy. That is not Rapture as claimed by the post tribulation Christians. In Revelation chapter 7, the One Hundred and Forty Four Thousand Jews with the seal of God on their heads and other too numerous to be counted will be translated or Raptured during the great tribulation as they can be seen before the throne in heaven (Revelation 7:9). They will be instrumental in preaching to their Jewish brethren so that the other Jews will accept Jesus as Lord and personal saviour and a nation will be born in a day and that nation will remain throughout the tribulation period and will be gathered from all over the world into Jerusalem in fulfillment of prophecy after the Great Tribulation.

Israel as it is today is not a Christian nation. So Israel will definitely miss the Rapture except for few of them that are born again. Other careless Christians too will miss the Rapture. But God is still very much interested in Israel being the first born (Exodus 4:22). They have a lot of roles to play in the end time agenda of God.

During the Great tribulation, the careless Christians who will by then realize that Jesus Christ is truly the Savior will not want to take the mark of the Beast and some of them will obtain salvation by their own blood. Israel will enter into an agreement with the Anti-Christ which will be terminated when they see the abomination that causes the desolation as foretold by Daniel and our Lord Jesus Christ in the middle of the tribulation period. So the whole nation of Israel shall repent in a single day. Please Read Zachariah 12:9-10; they shall look upon him whom they have pierced and the nation will become born again in a day (Romans 11:26).

Isaiah 66: 7-10 reads

7: Before she travailed she brought forth; before her pain came she was delivered of a man child,

8: Who hath heard such a thing? Shall the earth be made to bring forth in a day? Or shall a nation be born at once? For as soon as Zion travailed, she brought forth her children.

9: Shall I bring to the birth and not cause to bring forth? Saith the Lord; shall I cause to bring forth, and shut the womb? Saith thy God.

10: Rejoice ye with Jerusalem and be glad with her, all ye that love her; rejoice for joy with her all ye that mourn for her.

There are other people from other nations that will repent during the Great tribulation, these are the tribulation saints. It is for their sakes that the Great tribulation period will be shortened. During this time, as earlier mentioned the Twelve Thousand Israelites from each of the twelve tribes making One Hundred and Forty Four Thousand and others too numerous to be counted from the nations that shall be marked with the mark of God shall engage in the preaching of the Gospel. They cannot be killed because of the mark of God on them. After their assignment they shall be Raptured towards the end of the Great tribulation as earlier mentioned (Rev 7:9-17). But remember that the nation of Israel that was born in a day as a result of their efforts and all the converts from the nations will remain throughout the tribulation period, many also will be killed since they will refuse to renounce their faith in Christ. It is worthy of mention that the whole of chapter 24 of Matthew did not deal with the Rapture but the second return of Christ to earth which deals with the Jews while the Rapture only concerns theChurch.

The question for the post tribulation Christians is that how will they know when the Great tribulation will start so that they can start counting the Seven years? Some of them are claiming that the Great tribulation of the Church has already started. When?

So the Church will be Raptured ahead of the great tribulation to be with the Lord in the air.

WHAT ARE THE QUALIFICATIONS FOR THE RAPTURE?

Bible says in John 3:3, 5

3: Jesus answered and said unto him verily, verily, I say unto thee, except a man be born again, he cannot see the Kingdom ofGod.

5: Jesus answered, verily, verily; I say unto thee except a man is born of water and of the spirit, he cannot enter into the kingdom of God.

There is only one qualification that enables a man to qualify for the Rapture – Accept Jesus Christ as Lord and personal Savior and abide in Him.

The process of abiding is the process of holiness. When a man comes to Christ he automatically becomes righteous. It is worthy of note that righteousness was purchased on our behalf by Christ.

Righteousness is NOT our right standing before God; this is an erroneous definition of what righteousness is. Righteousness is Christ right standing before God on our behalf.

I Corinthians 5:21 says

21: For He (God) hath made him (Jesus) to be sin for us, who knew no sin; that we might be made the righteousness of God In Him (Jesus). *(*Emphasis is mine).

All our righteousness is just like a filthy rag before God. We only become righteous because of the righteousness of Christ before God. Hallelujah!

The analogy is very simple; a baby that is born today even without committing any sin is already a sinner, since he/she is a relation of Adam, in like manner a person that becomes born again today becomes righteous through Christ just by accepting Christ.

Being righteous only is not sufficient as we are admonished to work out our salvation with fear and trembling. Holiness must be the watch word for every believer. Holiness was NOT purchased for us, no. we have to work it out not work for it. 1 Peter 1:15 -16 says

15: But as He which hath called you is holy, so be ye holy in all manner of conversation;

16: Because it is written, be ye holy; for I am holy.

Holiness is therefore a performance which is required from the believer. Hebrew 12:14 says

14: Follow peace with all men, and holiness, without which no man shall see the lord.

In conclusion the condition for making the Rapture is to be born again and live a life of holiness

SEQUENCE OF EVENT

1. Jesus Christ is preparing a mansion for us and he will come back for us.

2. He will bring back to life those who are dead in Christ and give them a new body (a spiritual body with soul) when the trumpet sounds (I Thessalonians 4:16).

3. We who are still alive at His coming will be caught up together with the dead in Christ to meet with the Lord in the air (I Thessalonians.4:17).

4. This will all happen suddenly.

5. We will be with the Lord in the air for seven years

6. In the seven years, the world will suffer the great tribulation.

7. While in the air, we will appear before the judgment seat of Christ (not of the father) to give an account of ourselves while in the body and also receive rewards accordingly (II Corinthians.5:10)

8. Marriage supper of the lamb will take place; Christ

will be married to His bride (not the church). The brides of Christ are the old time saints and the redeemed Church (New Jerusalem). Rev 21:2, 9-11. The bride of Christ comprises of the old time saints and the Church, not just the Church.

The Rapture

CHAPTER THREE

47

THE THRONE OF GOD IN HEAVEN

O Lord Of Hosts, God Of Israel,

That Dwellest Between The Cherubims,
Thou Art The God, Even Thou Alone,
Of All The Kingdoms Of The Earth:
Thou Hast Made Heaven And Earth

Isaiah 37:16

THE THRONE OF GOD IN HEAVEN

Immediately after the events of the church in chapter 3, Apostle John was taken into the spirit to have a glimpse of the events in heaven. There in the third heaven is the throne of God and God was seated on His throne.

Round about the throne of God are twenty four seats and upon the twenty four seats are twenty four elders sitting, clothed in white apparels with crowns of gold upon their heads.

From the throne of God proceeded lightings which is very bright and there in the throne are seven lamps which are the seven spirits of God, just in front of the throne is a sea of glass which is as clear as crystal surrounded by four beasts full of eyes.

THE TWENTY FOUR ELDERS

The twenty four elders are not in heaven at the moment since this event is futuristic but from the scripture we can have an idea of who they are. At the time of their manifestation all that they will be doing is to worship God and cast their crowns before His throne.

SO WHO ARE THEY?

The twenty four elders are humans and not angels who clearly are believers who have been redeemed by the blood of Jesus. In Revelation chapter five, one of the elders came to Apostle John and told him that the risen Christ had the solution to a problem that nobody else could solve in heaven, earth or under the earth. When Christ resolved the issue the elders sang a song.

Revelation 5:9

9: And they sang a new song saying, thou art worthy to take the book, and to open the seals thereof: for thou was slain and has redeemed us to God by thy blood out of every kindred and tongue and people and nation.

The scripture clearly shows that the twenty four elders represent the Raptured church.

In Revelation 4:4 the *Bible says*

4: And round about the throne were four and twenty seats: and upon the seat I saw four and twenty elders sitting clothed in white raiment: and they had on their heads crowns of gold.

White raiment signified righteousness and redemption, while crowns are only won by human beings and not angels. Since this event is in revelation 4 and 5, it is a further proof that the Rapture is before the great tribulation since the event in chapter 4 and 5 occurred in Heaven and before the Great tribulation.

WHO ARE THE FOUR BEAST

The four beasts that were described in revelation 4 and 5 are in the higher category of angels in the class of cherubim. Their duty before God is to worship him at all times. These same four beasts that are eternal in nature are the same set of angels described as the four living creatures in Ezekiel 1:10.

10: As for the likeness of their faces, they four had the face of a man, and the face of a lion, on the right side: and they four had the face of an ox on the left side; they four also had the face of an eagle.

Compare this Scripture with Revelation 4:7-8.

It is very interesting to note that the four living beast or creatures demonstrated that Jesus Christ, the lamb of God is equal to God Himself, their worship of the lamb in Revelation 5:6-14 is directed to Jesus Christ.

In Revelation 5:13 the Bible says

13: And every creature which is in heaven and on the earth and under the earth and as such that are in the sea, and all that are in them, heard I saying, blessing and honor and glory and power be unto him that sitteth upon the throne and unto the lamb forever and ever.

THE SEVEN SPIRITS OF GOD BEFORE THE THRONE

Not so much is recorded in the Scripture about the seven Spirits of God which is referred to here. But it is certain that they exist. The seven Spirits are also referred to as the seven lamps (Zachariah 4:2). Wherever the seven are referred to, there is also a reference to illumination.

The seven spirits are believed to be held by the lord Jesus Christ. In Revelation 3:1, 4:5-6, Bible says

1: Unto the angel of the church in Sardis write; These things saith He that hath the seven spirits of God and the seven stars...

5: and out of the throne proceeded lightnings and thunderings and voices and there were seven lamps of fire burning before the throne which are the seven Spirits of God.

6: and before the throne there was a sea of glass like unto crystal: and in the midst of the throne and round about the throne were four beasts full of eyes before and behind. The seven spirits are the seven lamps which are also the seven eyes of the lamb.

According to Bible scholars, the seven Spirits of God could be what Isaiah was referring to in Isaiah 11:2

2: and the spirit of the lord shall rest upon

him, the spirit of wisdom and understanding, the spirit of counsel and might, the spirit of knowledge and of the fear of the Lord.

Since Jesus holds the seven spirits of God, these can be summarized as follows:

1. The spirit of the Lord

2. The spirit of wisdom

3. The spirit of understanding

4. The spirit of counsel

5. The spirit of might

6. The spirit of knowledge

7. The spirit of the fear of the Lord

These may be the seven spirits of God. The throne of God is a literal place. It is located in the third heaven by the side of the north. In Psalm 48:1-2, the Bible says

1; Great is the Lord, and greatly to be praised in the city of our God, in the mountain of his holiness.

2; Beautiful for situation, the joy of the whole earth is mount Zion on the side of the north the city of the great king.

Before the creation of the earth, God and his angels were living together in perfect harmony worshipping God and giving Him the glory.

Lucifer was the cherub that covers. He was made of different pipes of music. He was responsible for providing music for the worship of God until iniquity was found with him. Isaiah 14:12-14 says

12: How art thou fallen from heaven, O Lucifer, son of the morning! How art thou cut down to the ground, which didst weaken the nations!

13: for thou hast said in thine heart, I will ascend unto heaven, I will exalt my throne above the stars of God: I will sit also upon the mount of the congregation in the sides of the north.

14: I will ascend above the heights of the cloud; I will be like the most high.

The above Scripture clearly shows that the throne of God is literal and it is by the side of the north.

Since the ascension of Christ into heaven, He is seated at the right hand side of the father on His throne where He provides intercession on our behalf in the court of heaven where the accuser of the brethren accuses us daily before God. Romans 8:34says

34: Who is it that condemneth? It is Christ that died, yea rather, that is risen again, who

is even at the right hand of God, who maketh intercession forus.

Read also Hebrews 7:25

CHAPTER FOUR

55

THE TIMES OF THE GENTILES

And They Shall Fall By The Edge Of The Sword, And Shall Be Led Away Captive Into All Nations: And Jerusalem Shall Be Troden Down Of The Gentiles, Until The Times Of The Gentiles Be Fulfilled

Luke 21:24

THE TIMES OF THE GENTILES

WHICH PERIOD IS REFERRED TO AS THE TIMES OF THE GENTILES?

These times represent the period throughout the history of the Jews when they are under one captivity/oppression or the other. This period of oppression started in Egypt and will extend to the period immediately after the Great tribulation. It will climax under the leadership of the Anti-Christ, when he will break his 7 years agreement with Israel in the middle of the tribulation period. He will take over Jerusalem and the future Jewish temple as his capital building and he will perform the abomination that causes the desolation (Self worship). He will place his image in the temple and force people to worship it.

Daniel 9:27says

27: And he shall confirm the covenant with many for one week (seven years): and in the midst of the week, he shall cause the sacrifice and oblation to cease, and for the overspreading of abominations he shall make it desolate even until the consummation, and that determined shall be poured upon the desolate. (Emphasis is mine)

Read also Daniel 11:4-45.

This will continue for 42 months after the agreement has

been broken until the physical return of Jesus to earth to establish the millennium rule of one thousand years while the Anti-Christ and the false prophet will be cast alive into the lake of fire. This will signify the end of the times of the Gentiles. Revelation 11:1-2 says:

1: And there was given me a reed like unto a rod: and the angel stood, saying, Rise and measure the temple of God and the altar and them that worship therein.

2: But the court which is without the temple leave out, and measure it not, for it is given unto the Gentiles and the holy city shall they tread under forty and two months. (3 and half years). (Emphasis is mine).

This is further corroborated in the book of Zechariah 14:2-3 which says:

2: For I will gather all nations against Jerusalem to battle and the city shall be taken and the houses rifled, and the women ravished; and half of the city shall go forth into captivity, and the residue of the people shall not be cut off from the city.

3: Then shall the LORD go forth and fight against those nations, as when He fought in the day of battle.

So the times of the Gentiles are a period of times from the

Jews' first captivity in Egypt till the physical coming of the Lord Jesus Christ to deliver them after the great tribulations.

THE KINGDOMS THAT WILL OPPRESS ISRAEL IN THE TIMES OF THE GENTILES

There are eight kingdoms in the times of the Gentiles that will oppress Israel. Six have fulfilled prophecy; two more kingdoms are outstanding to the end of age (world)

1.   EGYPT

This is the first kingdom in the times of the Gentile to oppress Israel. Israel went into captivity when Joseph was sold into slavery. Joseph was the eleventh child of Jacob (Israel) born to him by his beloved wife Rachael. He loved Joseph above all the other eleven children. Rachael had only Joseph and Benjamin for Israel. Israel made a coat of many colors for his beloved son and wouldn't allow him to go to the field except to supervise his brothers.

The open love for him and his younger brother Benjamin above the other ten was so glaring. Above all, Joseph had some strange dreams which suggested that he was going to rule over the whole family including his father and mother. His father rebuked him sharply but his brothers took the dreams to heart to ensure that it will not be fulfilled. *For proper understanding read the whole of Genesis 37. In verses 26-27*

26: And Judah said unto his brethren, what profit is it if we slay our brother, and conceal

his blood?

27: Come and let us sell him to the Ishmaelite and let not our hand be upon him, for he is our brother and our flesh. And his brothers were content.

God eventually delivered Israel after staying in Captivity and oppression for four hundred and thirty years with very hard labor. Extra 30 years because nobody stood in the gap.

God brought out Israel by the strength of the hand of the LORD. Exodus 13:*3* says

3: And Moses said unto the people, remember this day, in which ye came out from Egypt out of the house of bondage; for by strength of the hand of the LORD brought you out from this place: there shall no leavened bread beeaten.

The captivity lasted for Four Hundred and Thirty years instead of Four Hundred years.

2: ASSYRIA

This is the second kingdom in the times of the Gentiles that oppressed Israel. Their oppression of Israel is scattered over a period of more than one thousand five hundred years.
This represents a period in the history of Israel and Judah during which several thousand Israelites of ancient

Samaria were settled as captives by Assyria. This is one of the many forceful relocation implemented by Neo Assyrian empires.

The Northern kingdom of Israel was conquered by the Neo Assyrian monarch Tiglath-Pilneser II and Shalmaneser V. Sargon II and Sennacherib were responsible for finishing twenty years demise of the northern ten tribes although the southern kingdom remained. Jerusalem was also besieged but not taken.

The tribes that were resettled by the force by the Assyrians were later referred to as the ten lost tribes.
The captivity started around 740 BCE.

In I Chronicles *5:26*

26: And the God of Israel stirred the spirit of Pul king of Assyria and the spirit of Tiglath-Pilneser King of Assyria and he carried them away even the Reubenites and the Gadites and the half tribe of Manasseh and brought them unto Halah and Habor and Hara and to the river Gozan unto this day.

II Kings 15:29 says

29: In the days of Rekah king of Israel came Tiglath-Pilneser king of Assyria and he took Ijon and Abel Beth and Maacah and Janoah and Kedesh and Hazor and Gilead and

Galilee, all the land of Napthali and carried them captives to Assyria.

In 722 BCE, ten to twenty years after the initial deportation, the ruling city of the Northern kingdom of Israel, Samaria was finally taken by Sargon II after a three year siege initiated by Shalmaneser V. (Read II kings 17:3-6)

The book of kings stated several times that the entire people of the kingdom of Israel had been taken into exile by the Assyrians. Each time the Jews repented, the LORD had mercy on them. Today Israel has outlived these enemies.

3: **BABYLON**:

This is the third kingdom in the times of the Gentiles to oppress Israel. The full account can be found in the book of Daniel, Jeremiah, Ezekiel etc. Most of the account here will be taken from the book of Daniel.

In Daniel 1:1-2, Bible says

1: In the third year of the reign of Jehoiakim king of Judah came Nebuchadnezzar king of Babylon unto Jerusalem and besieged it.

2: And the Lord gave Jehoiakim king of Judah into his hand, with part of the vessels of the house of God: which he carried into the

land of Shinar to the house of his god; and he brought the vessels into the treasure house of his god.

The event above was to last seventy years as prophesied by Jeremiah although because of the prayers of Daniel it lasted Sixty Eight years. This captivity was the most interesting of them all. It produced three Governors, a prime minister that eventually served five kings over a period of Sixty Eight years. It was also during this period that the Almighty God gave a very important vision to a heathen king; the vision had to do with the end time. It was also during this period that God gave a lot of very important visions to Daniel concerning the end time. The book of Daniel and Revelation are very similar with both discussing the manifestation of the Anti-Christ and his brutal hatred for Israel.

In Daniel chapter 2:1-end (please read), God gave a vision to Nebuchadnezzar, in the vision, he saw a great image with excellent brightness which stood before him made up of Gold, Silver, Brass, Iron and Clay. The vision frightened him and he knew that it was not just an ordinary dream.

He called in all the wise men of Babylon to narrate the dream to him and its interpretation; he didn't want to take any chance. The dream was taken away from him so there was no dream to relay to the wise men of Babylon but he knew there was a dream and a very important one at that. The only reasonable thing as far as he is concerned is that they should relay the dream to him and the interpretation also. Once the dream can be relayed, there wouldn't be any doubt that the interpretation was real.

Daniel 2:9-11 says

9: But if ye will not make known unto me the dream, there is but one decree for you: for ye have prepared lying and corrupt words to speak before me, till the time be changed; therefore tell me the dream and I shall know that ye can show me the interpretation thereof.

10: The Chaldeans answered before the king and said there is not a man upon the earth that can show the king's matter: therefore there is no king, Lord, nor ruler, that asked such things at any magician or astrologer or Chaldean.

11: And it is a rare thing that the king required and there is none other than can shew it before the king, except the gods, whose dwelling is not with flesh.

As far as the king was concerned if the vision was not made known to him as well as the interpretation, there is but one decree and that is to destroy the wise men of Babylon.

12: For this cause, the king was angry and very furious, and commanded to destroy all the wise men of Babylon

The wise men were being gathered for execution including Daniel and his friends when he enquired from the commander of the king's guard why the decree was so urgent. The commander of the King's guard explained the situation to Daniel and God provided the solution to Daniel in a dream.

The vision of Nebuchadnezzar was so significant because it foretells what will happen in the next 420 years and also at the end time especially as it concerns the Jews and 6 Kingdoms from that time to the end.

In the vision, the image head of fine gold represents Babylon or Nebuchadnezzar. After Babylon another kingdom represented by the breast and arm of silver will arise. This kingdom will be inferior to Babylon just like silver is inferior to gold. That kingdom is Medo-Persia. After the Medo-Persian kingdom, another kingdom whose belly and thigh are of brass will arise, that is the Grecian kingdom.

The Roman Empire represented by legs of iron shall arise and subdue the Grecian kingdom. All these are fulfilled already. Out of the Roman Empire represented by the 10 feet will arise 10 kings or kingdoms (future) that will come together for a short time and will eventually endorse the little horn or the Anti-Christ which is the 8th Kingdom in the times of the Gentiles.

4 MEDO – PERSIAN:

This is the fourth kingdom to oppress Israel in the times of the Gentiles and the second of the six kingdoms in the vision of Nebuchadnezzar. They ruled the world after Babylon. In the vision of the king; it was represented as stated earlier by the breast and two arms of silver. Silver is inferior to gold so is the kingdom of Medes and the Persians is inferior to Babylonian Kingdom not in terms of strength since they eventually over threw the Babylonians.

The king in Babylon had absolute powers, he could kill at will whereas the Medo- Persian empire ruled by decrees through a king. After all, Darius the King couldn't help Daniel whom he respected so much from being thrown into the Lion's den despite knowing that Daniel was not guilty as long as the decree has been signed with the royal signet.

God also gave Daniel a vision about this same empire. In Daniel 8:1-4. The ram with two horns in the passage stands for the Medo-Persian kingdom as confirmed to Daniel by angel Gabriel in verse20

20: The ram which thou sawest having two horns are the kings of Media and Persia.

They were eventually defeated by the Grecian Empire under the leadership of Alexander the Great.

5. GRECIA:

Daniel was not alive when the Grecian empire eventually manifested, but the vision was given to him. The Grecian empire conquered the Medo-Persian Empire in less than 13 years under the leadership of Alexander the great and became the fifth kingdom in the times of the Gentiles to rule the world and also to oppress Israel.

In the vision of the king, the kingdom is represented by the belly and thigh of brass, the kingdom is inferior to both the Babylonian and the Medo-Persiankingdoms.
In Daniel's vision in chapter 8, the Grecians Empire is represented by a He goat. Daniel 8:5-9 says

5: And as I was considering, behold, an he goat came from the west on the face of the whole earth, and touched not the ground: And the goat had a notable horn (Alexander the great) between his eyes

6: And he came to the ram that had two horns, which I had seen standing before the river and ran unto him in the fury of his power.

7: And I saw him come close unto the ram and he was move with choler against him, and smote the ram and break his two horns (Medes and Persian); and there was no power in the ram to stand before him, but he cast

him down to the ground and stamped upon him; and there was none that could deliver the ram out his hand.

8: Therefore the he-goat (Grecian Empire) waxed very great; and when he was strong, the great horn (Alexander the Great) was broken; and for it came up four notable ones (Cassandra, Lysimachus, Selecus and Ptolemy) towards the four winds of heaven.

9: and out of one of them came forth a little horn, which waxed exceeding great, toward the south, and toward the east, and toward the pleasantland. (Emphasis is mine).

Verse 5 speaks about the speed and swiftness with which Alexander defeated the then known world. Alexander died at the age of 33 and four short lived kingdoms emerged from the Grecian empire.

Those countries today are

1. Greece
2. Turkey
3. Syria (including Lebanon, Iran, Iraq and Levant)
4. Egypt

According to verse 9, the ANTICHRIST will **emerge** from one of the above countries. The Anti-Christ will not be a sitting American president or an influential American

since America is neither a part of the former Grecian empire nor the old Roman Empire.
Note: Alexander the Great was not defeated by any army. He died at thirty three after conquering the world in a space of thirteen years.

He had four generals under him:

1. Cassandra took (Greece and Macedon (west)
2. Lysimachus took Turkey and Thrace (North)
3. Selecus took modern state of Syria, Lebanon, Iraq and Iran (East)
4. Ptolemy took Egypt (South).

So the kingdom was literally divided toward the four winds of heaven (verse8)

6. ROME

This is the sixth kingdom in the times of the Gentiles to oppress Israel. They also represent the fourth kingdom in the vision of king Nebuchadnezzar represented by the iron leg. This kingdom is to be stronger than all the preceding kingdoms as iron is stronger than Gold, Silver and Brass.
Daniel 2:40 says

40: And the fourth kingdom shall be strong as iron; for as much as iron breaketh in pieces and subdueth all things: and as iron

that breaketh all things: and as iron that breaketh all these, shall it break in pieces and bruise.

The Roman Empire eventually conquered the four kingdoms that came out of the Grecian empire. Daniel 7:23 says

23: Thus he said, the fourth beast shall be the fourth kingdom upon the earth, which shall be divers from all kingdoms, and shall devour the whole earth and shall tread it down and break it in pieces.

When Christ was manifested, the world was under the Roman Empire. It was under the same empire that the Revelation was given to Apostle John. He described the kingdom as one of the seven heads of the dragon or a mountain apparently referring to a kingdom.

In Revelation 17:9- 10 Bible says

9: And here is the mind which hath wisdom. The seven heads are seven mountains, on which the woman sitteth.

10: and these are the seven kings; five are fallen and one is, and the other is not yet come; and when he cometh, he must continue a short space.

This was written during the Roman Empire. The five fallen

kings or kingdoms are:

1. Egypt
2. Assyria
3. Babylon
4. Medo-Persia
5. Grecia

It says and 'one is' referring to the Roman Empire that was ruling the world then which has now fallen. Six kingdoms from the eight kingdoms that will oppress/maltreat Israel in the times of the Gentiles have fulfilled prophecy. There are two kingdoms now outstanding that will oppress Israel prompting the Lord's final intervention for His people Israel. The two outstanding kingdoms will be discussed in the next chapter.

CHAPTER FIVE

73

THE SEVEN AND EIGHT KINGDOMS
IN THE GENTILES

And The Ten Horns Out Of This Kingdom
Are Ten Kings That Shall Arise And
Another Shall Rise After Them;

And He Shall Be Diverse From
The First And He Shall Subdue
The Kings

Daniel 7:24

THE SEVENTH AND EIGHT KINGDOMS IN THE TIMES OF THE GENTILES

7. THE FUTURE KINGDOMS/KINGS

This is represented by the ten feet made up of mixture of iron and clay in the vision of Nebuchadnezzar. This is the seventh kingdom in the times of the Gentiles to oppress Israel. The kingdom will be partly strong since it is made partly of iron and partly weak since it is partly made of clay. The iron part will have dominion over the clay part. These ten kingdoms/Kings will come out of the former Roman Empire. In the vision of Daniel it was represented by ten horns.

In Daniel7:20 Bible says

20: And of the ten horns that were in his head, and of the other which came up, and before whom three fell; even of that horn that had eyes, and a mouth that spake very great things, whose look was more stout than his fellows.

It was further explained to Daniel, that the ten horns are ten future kings that will eventually produce the Anti-Christ. The ten future kings will come out of the revised Roman Empire and part of the Grecian Empire as earlier explained.

Daniel 7:24 says

24: And the ten horns out of this kingdom are ten kings that shall arise: and another shall rise after them; and he shall be diverse from the first and he shall subdue three Kings.

The Lord Jesus Christ revealed the vision to Apostle John which is exactly what the angel explained to Daniel. Revelation 17:12 says

12: And the ten horns which thou sawest are ten kings which have received no kingdoms as yet; but receive power as kings ONE hour with the Beast. Emphasis is mine.

Revelation 17: 10 says

10: and there are seven kings: five are fallen (Egypt, Assyria, Babylon, Medo-Persia, Greece) and one is (Rome at the time of Apostle john) and the other is not yet come (Ten future kings); And when he cometh, he must continue a short space (One prophetic hour). (Emphasis is mine).

The one hour is a prophetic one hour not literal. From Scriptural calculations, that prophetic one hour comes to seven months ten days. How was this figure arrived at? In Daniel 8:13-14, Bible says

13: Then I heard one saint speaking and another saint said unto that certain saint

which spake, how long shall be the vision concerning the daily sacrifice and the transgression of desolation to give both the sanctuary and the host to be trodden under foot (The great tribulation)?

14: And he said unto me, unto two thousand and three hundred days; then shall the sanctuary becleansed. (Emphasis is mine).

The great tribulation is seven years which is 2,520 days. The Anti-Christ according to verse 14 will reign for 2,300 days.

The ten future kings who will receive the power for a short space immediately after the Rapture to control things because of the confusion that will arise, they will then reign for 2,520 days minus 2,300 days. This will amount to 220 days or effectively 7 months 10 days (short space of time or the prophetic ONE Hour). They will hand over to the Anti-Christ who will reign for 6 years four month and 20 days. Hallelujah.

8. THE ANTI-CHRIST OR THE LITTLE HORN (THE BEAST)

The Anti-Christ is described in Scripture as the man of lawlessness, man of sin, son of perdition (II Thessalonians 2:3), he will rule over the world during the time of the Great tribulation and he will be the last ruler in the times of the Gentiles. It is towards the end of his rule that Jesus

Christ will physically come down to earth and overthrow him at the seventh year of the end of this age(Last seven years of this age).

He will be the most wicked ruler that has ever transverse the globe. What other wicked rulers like Adolf Hitler, Benito Mussolini, king Nero did in the past, will all amount to a child's play compared to what the man of lawlessness will do. During his reign, wickedness shall be taken to a new dimension. It shall be a demonic marshal law with people's rights completely withdrawn.

He will be a product of the defunct Grecian empire which will be a city under the ten future kings which will receive power in the future or the revived Roman Empire.

Daniel 8:8-10 *says*

8: Therefore the he goat (Grecian empire) waxed very great: and when he was strong the great horn (Alexander the great) was broken; and for it came up four notable ones towards the four winds of heaven.

9: And out of one of them came forth a little horn (the Anti-Christ) which waxed exceeding great toward the south and towards the east, and towards the pleasantland.

10: And it waxed great, even to the host of heaven; and it cast down some of the host and

of the stars to the ground and stamped upon them. Emphasis is mine.

Read also Revelation 17:1-end.

The Anti-Christ will be manifested as a strong political and economic leader with very powerful military Capabilities. He will initially be presented as a man of peace to the world, since the world is desperately looking for peace, the world will readily accept him at his manifestation.

In Revelation 6:1-2, he can be seen riding on a white horse, symbolizing a man of peace. He was also holding a bow without an arrow signifying conquest without war. A man of great diplomacy that will bring peace to Israel and its neighbors. This has never happened but will happen only during his reign.

He will sign a peace pact of seven years with Israel and break the pact three and half years later.

In Daniel 9:27 Bible says

27: And he shall confirm the covenant with many for one week (7 years): and in the midst of the week he shall cause the sacrifice and the oblation to cease and for the overspreading of abominations he shall make it desolate, even until the consummation and that determined shall

be poured upon the desolate.

The Anti-Christ will take over the temple in Jerusalem and demand worship from all humanity and will brutally execute anyone that does not worship him. (Revelation13:14). And for almost seven years the world will witness the kind of wickedness that has never happened before. At the end of the seven years, the Lord Jesus Christ will defeat him and throw him alive into the lake of fire.

Revelation 19:20 says

20: And the beast was taken, and with him the false prophet that wrought miracles before him, with which he deceived them that had received the mark of the beast and them that worshipped his image. These both were cast alive into a lake of fire burning with brimstone.

That marks the end of the times of the Gentiles and the restoration of the people of God. The Anti-Christ will manifest any moment; the presence of the Church is what is withholding his manifestation.

I Thessalonians *2:7* says that he that withholds will continue to withhold, until it will be taken out of the way. He that withholds is the church and Not the Holy Spirit as some claim. It is a blasphemy to say that the Holy Spirit will be taken away. The Holy Spirit is God and he is

Omnipresent.

After the pact is broken and Israel is seriously persecuted along with other careless Christians who will miss the Rapture, the whole of Israel will become saved in a day knowing that the Anti-Christ (Beast) is not the Messiah.

Isaiah 66:7-9says

7: Before she travailed, she brought forth; before her pain came she was delivered of a man child.

8: Who hath heard such a thing? Who hath seen such things? Shall the earth be made to bring forth in one day? Or shall a nation be born at once? For as soon as Zion travailed, she brought forth her children.

9: Shall I bring to the birth and not cause to bring forth? Saith the Lord: shall I cause to bring forth and shut the womb? Saith thy God

Romans 11:25-26 says

25: For I would not, brethren that ye should be ignorant of this mystery, lest ye should be wise in your own conceit; That blindness in part is happened to Israel, until the fullness of <u>the Gentiles</u> be come in,

26: And so all Israel shall be saved; as it is written, there shall come out of Zion the deliverer and shall turn away ungodliness from Jacob: emphasis is mine.

CHAPTER SIX

THE FALSE TRINITY

And I Saw Three Unclean Spirits Like Frogs Come Out Of The Mouth Of The Dragon And Out Of The Mouth

Of The Beast, And Out Of The Mouth Of The False Prophet

Revelation 16:13

THE FALSE TRINITY

And no marvel; for Satan himself is transformed into an angel of light – II Corinthians 11:14.

During the seven years of the reign of the Anti-Christ, the trio of Satan (the dragon), the Anti-Christ and the false prophet will be ruling together on earth, although they will not be fully in control. They will constitute the unholy trinity. Satan the dragon will play the role of the false father; the Anti Christ (Beast) will play the role of the false son while the false prophet will play the role of the false "holy spirit".

After Satan rebelled against God in heaven before the creation of man, he was expelled with one third of the angels that are loyal to him. His service to God was terminated and his office given to other higher angels. Satan and his demons became wandering spirits, the demons were disembodied, meaning they cannot operate on their own without possessing the bodies of humans, animals or trees. Satan as at today (20/04/2020) is still allowed in the court of God in heaven where he accuses the brethren before God.

In the book of Job when the sons of God (the angels) were meeting with God to present themselves before Him, Satan also made an appearance. He is allowed in the court but not allowed in any type of fellowship, he goes to and fro the earth as a fugitive and a vagabond looking for those to accuse before God. Please read Job chapters 1 and 2.

Just immediately after the Rapture all the privileges of access to heaven will be denied the devil. The devil will resist not being granted access, this will result in a war the second time. Michael will be called upon to once again humiliate Satan just like he did to him when iniquity was found in him.

Michael will successfully prosecute the war and banish Satan to the earth. Satan will come to the earth with great anger knowing that his time is short.

Revelation 12:7-10, 12 says

7: And there was war in heaven: Michael and his angels fought against the dragon; and the dragon fought and his angels,

8: And prevailed not; neither was their place found any more in heaven.

9: And the great dragon was cast out that old serpent, called the Devil and Satan, which deceiveth the whole world: he was cast out into the earth, and his angels were cast out with him.

10: And I heard a loud voice saying in heaven now is come salvation, and strength and the kingdom of our God, and the power of His Christ: for the accuser of our brethren is cast down,

which accused them before our God day and night.

12: Therefore rejoice ye heavens and ye that dwell in them. Woe to the inhabiters of the earth and of the sea for the devil is come down unto you, having great wrath, because he knoweth that he hath but a short time.

The above Scriptures clearly shows that the event mentioned above is in the future, during the seven years reign, Satan will be here on earth to head the false trinity in conjunction with the Beast and the false prophet, this is the reason why the reign of the Beast will be a very brutal reign with wickedness such as never seen before.

(A)   WHO IS SATAN?

Satan is referred to as the serpent, dragon, accuser of the brethren, god of this world, the devil etc. he was originally named Lucifer, the anointed cherub that covers the throne of God. God created him and gave him superior wisdom, he was perfect in beauty, a workmanship of every precious stone and pipes (music), perfect in his ways like other angels until he rebelled against God and was humiliated.

Isaiah 14:12-14*says*

12: How art thou fallen from heaven, O Lucifer, son of the morning! How art thou cut down to the ground, which didst weaken the nations!

13: For thou have said in thine heart, I will ascend into heaven; i will exalt my throne above the stars of God: I will sit also upon the mount of the congregation, in the sides of the North:

14: I will ascend above the heights of the clouds; I will be like the most High.

Also in Ezekiel, a description of Satan is given.

Ezekiel 28:12-15 *says*

12: Son of man, take up a lamentation upon the king of Tyrus, and say unto him, thus saith the Lord God; Thou sealest up the sum, full of wisdom, and perfect in beauty.

13: Thou has been in Eden the garden of God; every precious stone was thy covering, the sardius, topaz, and the diamond, the beryl, the onyx, and the jasper, the sapphire, the emerald, and the carbuncle, and gold; the workmanship of thy tabret and of thy pipes was prepared in thee in the day that thou was created.

14: Thou art the anointed cherub that covereth; and I have set thee so: thou was upon the holy mountain of God; thou hast walked up and down in the midst of the stones offire.

15: Thou was perfect in thy ways from the day that thou was created, till iniquity was found in thee.

Satan is a deceiver. He was the one that deceived our first parents in order to distort the plan of God for man. His plan is to take so many people to hell. Christ defeated him at the cross by disarming and dethroning him. He will yet defeat him finally at the end of the age.

Satan subtly took over dominion from Adam; he had a reign of terror from the time of Adam to Christ through his perverse wisdom. He tempted Jesus trying to offer Him a bribe to forsake redemption. The plan failed. He went through the Jews to crucify Jesus thinking that will finally truncate the plan of God, but in the death of Jesus lies the defeat of the devil. Glory to God! Revelation 1:17-18 says

17: And when I saw Him, I fell at his feet as dead. And He laid His right hand upon me, saying unto me, fear not; I am the first and the last.

18: I am he that liveth, and was dead; and behold, I am alive for evermore, Amen; and have the keys of hell and death.

At their final appointment in the future, Christ will condemn him to eternal damnation. Glory to God.

(B)   THE ANTI-CHRIST (BEAST)

OR FALSE SON?

So much has been said about the Beast in this book. He is called the man of lawlessness, the man of sin, the son of perdition, the Beast etc. Like it is said here earlier, the Beast is a human being and not a demon or a Satan's incarnate as thought in some quarters. He will have political, economic and military power.

In the Initial part of his reign, he will bring peace to many troubled spots in the world including the Middle East.

The Beast will control trade and commerce from the center and also try to keep a tab on everybody on earth by giving them a MARK through the use of advanced technology which we already have today and still being improved; the MARK is certainly going to be a CHIP IMPLANT connected to a data base in a computer. The CHIP will have all the information of the recipient captured in it. This is already being demonstrated in some countries. The CHIP will be on the right hand or on the fore head. Without the MARK, nobody will be able to buy or sell or do any transaction just like it is impossible to do any banking transaction in some countries without the Bank Verification Number(BVN).

The MARK will be used for all form of access including: markets, schools, hospitals, banks, public transportation systems etc. It will become almost impossible to live without it. The Beast will FORCE people to take the MARK or be brutally killed by his soldiers; he will be so powerful (Revelation 13:2) because his powers will be directly from the devil blaspheming God at every given opportunity. Daniel 8:24 says he will make war against Israel and defeat them and other countries too, many of whom will resist him, at a time he will sustain a mortal wound that almost killed him, it eventually healed leaving the world in utter surprise (Revelation 13:3).

He will set himself in the temple at Jerusalem and demand worship from the whole world. Whosoever, whose name is not written in the book of the Lamb will obtain the MARK and worship him. The MARK means eternal damnation. At the end of the seven years, Christ will come and arrest him sending him alive into his final destination which is the lake of fire.

Revelation 19:20 says

20: And the Beast was taken, and with him the false prophet that wrought miracles before him, with which he deceived them that had received the mark of the Beast, and them that worshiped his image. These both were cast alive into a lake of fire burning with brimstone.

Note: It is not just the MARK that will be in operation. There are three options:

1.   The mark of the beast

2.   The name of the beast
3.   The number of his name (666)

Ensure you repent today so that you will not miss the first flight which is the Rapture.

(C)   THE FALSE PROPHET OR THE FALSE "HOLY SPIRIT"

The false prophet is the third personality that will reign with the devil and the Beast, he will also exercise all the powers of the Beast, working out fake miracles and enforcing the orders and the mandate of the Beast.
Just like the Beast, he is also a man, a human being probably with a strong religious background and influence. He will be in charge of the apostate religion of the Beast worship.

Revelation 13:11-15 says
11: And I beheld another beast coming up out of the earth; and he had two horns like a lamb, and he spake as a dragon.

12: And he exerciseth all the power of the first beast before him, and causeth the earth and them which dwell therein to worship the first beast whose deadly wound was healed.

13: And he doeth great wonders, so that he maketh fire come down from heaven on the earth in the sight of men.

14: And deceiveth them that dwell on the earth by the means of those miracles which he had power to do in the sight of the beast; saying to them that dwell on the earth, that they should make an image to the beast, which had the wound by a sword, and did live.

15: And he had power to give life unto the image of the beast, that the image of the beast should both speak and cause that as many as would not worship the image of the beast should be killed.

Observe that in verse 11, the Bible speaks about his appearance. He appeared like a lamb which is the most harmless animal, meaning he also will start like a man of peace too, probably with a great religious pedigree but he will eventually speak like a dragon (the devil). He will be the enforcer of the mandate of the first Beast (the Anti-Christ). He is likely to be a very big religious leader, trusted by many. After the seven years of the great tribulation, he will be defeated by the LORD JESUS CHRIST and Christ will cast him into the lake of fire where he will be tormented day and night. Please read Revelation 19.

Their mode of operation is clearly like the operation of the blessed Trinity. Whatever God does, Satan has a way of trying to replicate it. But remember that Satan is fake from eternity to eternity.

.

CHAPTER SEVEN

THE GREAT TRIBULATION

Alas For That Day Is Great So That None Is Like It: It Is Even The Time Of Jacob's Trouble But He Shall Be Saved Out Of It

Jeremiah 30:7

THE GREAT TRIBULATION

The great tribulation is for a period of seven years. This will begin immediately after the Rapture of the Church. It is divided into two major parts.

a. The Lesser tribulation period
b. The Great tribulation period

Each of the periods will last for three and half years apart with the seven months and ten days(prophetic ONE HOUR) forming a part of the Lesser tribulation period. Immediately after the Rapture, ten kings or presidents will emerge with their kingdoms or countries. The little horn will emerge from the ten kingdoms or countries. Before the emergence of the Beast, the ten kings or presidents will rule together for a short period of time as mentioned in chapter four, they will rule for a period of 7 month 10 days. They will be the ones to form the new world religion, the new world government and a new global currency e.t.c

The movement for the new world religion is already in force. The major religions are coming together under the guise of seeking peace. Most of them believe that they are serving the same God so why the difference and violence permeating them? Eventually they will become one and will be ecumenical in nature; it will work to persecute Israel and Christians Who Missed the Rapture.

They will also seek to form a single central government something close to the European union but much more stronger. The idea is to be able to control everything including commerce from the centre. It requires a centralized rule-making authority, a hierarchy of institutions with universal membership. The constituent nations/kingdoms will cede their authority to one after three others kings or presidents would have been defeated. The other six will cede their powers to one voluntarily (the Beast).

In the seven months, they will also produce a single world currency which will be digital in nature. That single currency wouldn't be subject to exchange rate fluctuation because there will be no competing currencies to exchange against it, there will be no currency risk in international trade since the world would have been reduced to a global village. All transaction costs related to international finance would be eliminated. Exchanging currencies always requires a conversion which banks charge a fee for and there can be a loss in value in changing one currency to another. Once the global currency is put in place, all the above risks, costs etc would be eliminated.

As it is today, the World health organization (WHO) through some sponsors are making claims that the use of paper currency can easily spread the corona virus. There is a plan already towards changing into digital currency in preparation for the emergence of the Beast. The Corona virus is not a coincidence, it might have been carefully planned to fulfill a mandate. From basic scientific knowledge, viruses are non-living organism, basically enzymes or protein covered with a layer of fat. Unlike bacteria which are living organisms, viruses are created. Things will certainly never remain the same again after this copvid-19 pandemic.

All the conditions for the manifestation of lawlessness are in place, once the Church is Raptured, then the Beast emerges, the system will not be new to the world.

After 7 months and ten days, authority will be given to the little horn (the Beast) who will begin his 6 years 4 months and twenty days reign.

Daniel 7:8, 8:9-12, Revelation 13:2. Immediately after his manifestation, he will destroy the system that brought him in so that he can be an absolute or maximum ruler.

He will make a seven year peace agreement with Israel and her enemies (Daniel 9:26-27). But in the middle of the seven years, he will break the agreement by moving to Jerusalem, take over the temple, make it his headquarters and wage war against Israel and Christians and begin to rule the wholeworld *(Revelation 13:1-10).*

He will put a stop to all the activities in the temple; he will set up his image there and demands that he should be worshipped. Believers will be imprisoned and brutally murdered (martyred). Jeremiah 30:7 says

7: Alas for that day is great, so that none is like it: it is even the time of Jacob's trouble but he shall be saved out of it.

The second part of the Great tribulation begins with his several conquests, including the conquest of Israel. As the beast is persecuting believers and Israel, God will also punish the earth and unbelievers. So the Beast is not fully in charge. The earth will be punished with the seven seals, seven trumpets and seven vials (bowls) of God's wrath.

SEALS

THE FOUR HORSES (REVELATION 6)

God revealed to John the series of judgments to be unleashed upon the earth.

The first four seals are explained as four different horses andriders.

1. **First Seal** (Rev 6:1-2): WHITE HORSE- Horses in the Scripture are typically associated with triumph, majesty, power and conquest. The first horse is white, typically what a conquering king would ride into a city that he just defeated. The rider wears a crown, carries a bow but no arrows. This clearly

indicates that though he is a warrior, he didn't win by force but through peace. This rider is the Beast. Daniel 8:25 says

25: And through his policy also he shall cause craft to prosper in his hand; and he shall magnify himself in his heart and by <u>peace</u> shall destroy many; he shall also stand up against the Prince of princes; but he shall be broken without hand.

The rider (the Beast) will be given his crown by a world that elected him to bring about the peace and safety they desperately crave for.
This will eventually turn out to be a false peace.

2. **Second Seal** (Revelation 6:3-4): RED HORSE- The false peace is taken away when the red horse manifests, The Beast will start fighting war and several bloodshed will follow. A great sword was given to him to prosecute the war and he went forth and conquered.

3. **Third Seal** (Revelation 6: 5-6): BLACK HORSE- The black horse represents very horrible famines that will come upon the earth. The scales carried by the rider on the black horse represent a measuring system that will give a person barely enough to eat. Food will probably cost 8-10 times the normal cost. Whenever there is war, people

cannot farm as most people are displaced. This is clearly a situation of famine.

4. **Fourth Seal** (Revelation 6:7-8): PALE HORSE- Death is what will naturally happen when the above three situations occur. Death is the natural result of war and famine with hell or Hades following, meaning that as death occurs people are buried.

   25 percent of the population of the earth will be killed as a result of the four horses or seals. No wonder Jesus said in Matthew 24:21 that the tribulation period is a time that the world has never experienced before. This is just the beginning of Gods judgment.

5. **Fifth Seal** (Revelation 69-11)MARTYRS- When the fifth seal was opened, there under the altar of God are the souls of the tribulation believers who were martyred (murdered) for their believe in Christ. They were calling out to God for revenge on the people upon the earth. White robes were given to all of them and God promised them revenge once the numbers of those to be martyred are complete.

6. **Sixth Seal** (Revelation 6:12-14): When the sixth seal was opened, there occurred a great earth quake; the sun became darkened and the moon became as

blood. The stars of heaven fell to the earth.

7. **Seventh seal** (Revelation 8: 1- 5): The seventh seal contains the seven trumpets which represents another set of punishment to be unleashed by God upon the inhabitants of the earth.

TRUMPETS

1. **First trumpet** (Revelation 8: 7): When the first angel blew his trumpet, hails mingled with blood were cast upon the earth resulting in the destruction of one third of the earth's vegetation. This will lead to hunger and famine.

2. **Second Trumpet** (Revelations 8:8-9): When the second angel blew his trumpet, a great mountain burning with fire was thrown into the sea, turning one third of the sea into blood. This resulted in the death of onethird of all the aquatic animals and the destruction of one third of all the ships. This will cause great financial losses to people on earth especially the maritime industry.

3. **Third Trumpet** (Revelation 8: 10-11) When the third angel blew his trumpet, a great star fell from heaven blazing like a torch. The name of the star is warm wood and it fell upon one third of all the rivers and fountains turning waters into warm wood which made the waters to become very bitter. Whosoever drank the water died.

4. **Fourth Trumpet** (Revelation 8:12): When the fourth angel blew his trumpet, the sun, moon and the stars lost one third of their lights so that one third of the time in which they shone were darkened, This is very similar to what happened in the land of Egypt. Three more dangerous plagues were still to come upon the earth and its

inhabitants.

5. **Fifth Trumpet** (Revelation 9:1-11): When the fifth trumpet was blown by the fifth angel, a star fell from heaven. This star is likely to be an angel based on the personal pronoun "he" that was used for him. He will descend from heaven to open the abyss which is the future home of Satan for a thousand years. There he will liberate the creatures that will fulfill this judgment on the people on earth. This angel is likely to be a trusted angel since he holds the key to abyss. Immediately abyss was opened, out of it came smoke as great as the smoke of a furnace which darkened the sun and the air.

Then came out creatures like locust, they look like horses prepared for battle. They had on their head crowns of gold and their faces were like that of men but having long hair like women and teeth like that of a lion. On their chest is a breast plate of iron their tails like the tails of a scorpion. They operated under a king who is also the angel (demon) of the bottomless pit whose name in Hebrew is Abaddon or Apollyon in Greek. Their responsibility is to sting men who have not the seal of God in their forehands. They are also not permitted to hurt vegetation. In those five months men will seek death but shall not find it as a result of their torment. Death will flee away from men in those five months. One woe is past.

6. **Sixth Trumpet** (Revelation 9:12-13): When the sixth angel blew his trumpet, he was mandated to loosen the four angels tied by the great river Euphrates. They have been prepared to carry out this destruction. Their preparation was for a period of one year, one month, one day and one hour to kill one third of mankind who didn't have the seal of God. They were two hundred million in number. They will attack from the top of horses or probably a high tech military hardware which John didn't have words to describe. The horses had heads of lions and out of their mouths issued fire, smoke and brimstone.

One third of the population of the earth will die during this period from fire, smoke and brimstone. Their power is in their mouth and in their tales, for their tales resembles snakes and with their heads they will hurt people. By this time, half of the population of the earth would have died. The people who survived the woe, refused to repent from their evil ways and wickedness. This is an indication that there will still be opportunity to repent for those who miss the Rapture. But it is very foolish for anybody to take chances. Why not accept Jesus Christ now so that you will not partake in the Great tribulation?

7. **Seventh Trumpet**: (Revelation 15:1-8): The seventh trumpet ushered in the seven golden vials which contains the wrath of God on the

inhabitant of the earth.

Revelation 16:11 *says*

> **11: And I heard a great voice out of the temple saying to the seven angels, go your ways and pour out the vials of the wrath of God upon the earth.**

VIALS

1. **First Vial** (Revelation 16:2): The first angel poured out his vial upon the earth, a grievous sore with a very terrible odor fell upon the men which had the mark of the beast and upon them that worshipped his image.

2. **Second Vial** (Revelation 16: 3): The second angel poured his vial upon the sea, the sea turned into blood just like the blood of a dead man. The resultant effect is the death of all aquatic animals. This is the end of all aquatic animals

3. **Third Vial** (Revelation 16:4): And the third angel poured his vial upon the rivers and fountains of water, it turned into blood leaving the world with practically no source of water to drink. God is a righteous judge who has judged the earth by giving them blood to drink because they have shed the blood of the saints and prophets. The judgments are now coming in very quick succession.

4. **Fourth Vial** (Revelation 16:8-9): The fourth angel poured his vial into the sun and he was given power to scotch men with fire. Because of the great pains from the torment men blasphemed God instead of repenting from their evil deeds and wickedness

5. **Fifth Vial** (Revelation 16:10-11): The fifth angel poured his vial upon the throne of the Beast, his kingdom immediately went into an unusual darkness and the people felt a persistent discomfort. Yet again they blasphemed God for their pains and sores that caused them so much discomfort.

6 **Sixth vial** (Revelation 16:12-16): The sixth angel poured out his vial upon the great river Euphrates, the river became dry immediately preparing way for the kings of the east for the battle of Armageddon where the Antichrist (the Beast) and the false prophet will meet their water loo.

The culmination of God's wrath is the gathering together of all the Antichrist' forces along with all their remaining armies into a singular location where God will destroy them. The location is Jerusalem. Read Zachariah 14:2-4.

An army will come from the rising of the sun. A massive oriental invasion of Israel is thus prepared by God and aimed directly at the Antichrist base of operation. The oriental army is cajoled into acting along with other military legions around the world by the three frog like demonic spirits that proceeded from the mouth of the false prophet, the Antichrist and Satan himself. All the world armies will be convinced to converge on Israel because of the miracles performed by the false trinity. Christ will consume them with the splendor of his coming.

Revelation 19:19 says:

19: And I saw the Beast and the kings of the earth and their armies gathered together to make war against him that sat on the horse and against HIS army.

7. Seventh Vial: (Revelation 16:17-21): The seventh angel poured his vial into the air. This resulted in thunders and lightenings and eventually a great earthquake which will divide Jerusalem into three parts and caused the city of all countries to fall apart. Babylon will also come into remembrance.

Under this seventh vial, stones weighing about 114 pounds shall fall upon men. This vial will also put an end to the presence of every Island and mountains on earth.

CHAPTER EIGHT

THE MINISTRY OF THE TWO AND OTHER MYSTERIES

Then Said He, These Are The Two Anointed Ones, That Stand By The Lord Of The Whole Earth.

Zechariah 4:14

THE MINISTRY OF THE TWO WITNESSES AND OTHER MYSTERIES

REVELATION 11:3-5

3: And I will give power unto my two witnesses, and they shall prophesy a thousand two hundred and three score days, clothed in sackcloth.

4: These are the two olive trees, and the two candlesticks standing before the God of the earth.

5: And if any man will hurt them, fire proceeded out of their mouth and devoured their enemies: and if any man will hurt them he must in this manner bekilled.

The essence of this chapter is to determine who these two witnesses will be. A hint is given about them in Revelation 11: 4 which is also in the Old Testament.

In Zachariah 4:11-14 *Bible says*

11*:* Then answered I, and said unto him, what are these two olive trees upon the right side of the candlestick and upon the left side thereof?

12: And I answered again and said unto him, what be these two olive branches

which through the two golden pipes empty the golden oil out of themselves?

13: And he answered me and said, knowest thou not what these be? And I said, No my Lord.

14: Then said he, these are the two anointed ones that stand by the LORD of the whole earth.

It is very certain that the two Scriptures above taken from the Old and the New Testament are referring to the same persons. They are referred to in both Scriptures as the two Olive trees, the two candle sticks. And in Zechariah 4:14, an additional description is given. They are the two anointed ones that stand by the LORD of the whole earth.

WHO ARE THESE TWO WITNESSES

There are about three schools of thought on who these witnesses are likely to be. Some are of the opinion that they are Moses and Enoch. Some think that they are Elijah and Enoch. While some others believe that they are two future prophets who will come and prophesy for 42 months towards the end of the reign of the Beast. From the three views above and especially from the first two, Enoch is recurring.

1.   MOSES ANDENOCH

Why it cannot be a combination of Moses and Enoch is the fact that Moses is dead.

Joshua 1:1-2 says

1: Now after the death of Moses the servant of the LORD it came to pass that the LORD spoke unto Joshua the son of Nun, Moses' minister, saying,

2: Moses my servant is dead; now therefore arise, go over this Jordan, thou and all these people, unto the land which I do give to them, even to the children of Israel.

It is clear from Scripture that Moses died and since Christianity does not in any way support reincarnation, Moses can't possible come in the future since he is dead.

Hebrews 9:27 says

27: And as it appointed unto men once to die, but after this judgment.

Once a man dies, the next thing is judgment. The appearance of Moses and Elijah at the mount of transfiguration does not prove anything. It was just a vision of heaven which God gave to the three Apostles which is a proof that the soul is living and that Moses representing the law and Elijah representing the prophets are both loyal to Christ.

2. ELIJAH AND ENOCH

Elijah was taken into heaven in a chariot of fire.

In II Kings 2:11 Bible says

11: And it came to pass, as they still went on, and talked, that behold, there appeared a chariot of fire and horses of fire, and parted them both asunder; and Elijah went up by a whirlwind into heaven.

Elijah was given the honor of travelling into heaven with God's means of transportation and he is with God in heaven in his natural flesh. (Please read Nahum 1:3). **Malachi 4:5 says:**

5: Behold I will send you Elijah the prophet before the coming of the great and dreadful days of the Lord:

Elijah feeds into one of the two witnesses.

ENOCH: In Hebrews 11:5, the Bible says

5: By faith Enoch was translated that he should not see death; and was not found because God had translated him: for before his translation he had this testimony, that he pleasedGod.

Enoch is in heaven in the flesh just likeElijah. But because flesh and blood cannot inherit the kingdom of God (1 Corinthians 15:50), they will both come for a future assignment. During the reign of the Anti-Christ, both will be actively involved in evangelizing the Jews and the people of the nations; they will do that for 42 months. If anyone attempts to kill them, fire will come out of their mouths as of old and devour their enemies.

During the period of their 42 months ministerial assignment, they will become a very big thorn in the flesh of the false trinity especially the Anti-Christ who has proclaimed himself to be God. Many will wonder and probably ask the Anti Christ why he could not destroy them as any attempt will result in their enemies being devoured byfire.

The two witnesses will cause untold hardship to the followers of the Beast. Because in the days of their prophecy, they will have power to turn water into blood and smite the earth with plagues as often as they want. The world would experience so much trouble in their days. Once they are through with their 42 months assignment, Satan will wage war against them and defeat them in the city of Jerusalem. Their bodies will not be buried but left in the open so that the world can see their bodies and rejoice sending gifts to one another.

After 3 and half days, the Spirit of life from God will enter into them prompting them to rise on their feet while the whole world is watching through televisions, whatsApp or any modern technology of the time driven by the internet. A great voice will come from heaven which will be heard by all their enemies all over the world saying come up hither; Immediately they will come back to life and be Raptured (Taken up into Heaven) in the sight of all.

CHAPTER NINE

THE SECOND COMING – PAROUSIA

And When He Had Spoken These Things,
While They Beheld, He Was Taken Up; And
A Cloud Received Him Out Of Their Sight
And While They Looked Steadfastly Toward Heaven As
He Went Up, Behold,
Two Men Stood By Them
In White Apparel;
Which Also Said, Ye Men Of Galilee, Why Stand Ye Gazing
Up Into Heaven?
This Same Jesus,

Which Is Taken Up From You Into Heaven,
Shall So Come In Like Manner As
Ye Have Seen Him Go Into Heaven.

Acts 1:9-11

THE SECOND COMING – PAROUSIA

Just like Jesus Christ went into heaven physically, so shall his physical return be. He left into heaven from the Mount of Olives in Jerusalem and will also come back on mount olives in Jerusalem. This is the second coming of Jesus Christ and every eyes shall see him at His coming including those who pierced him.

The two men who wore white clothing at his ascension are angels who were telling the people not to worry because he will return in the same manner he left. Their word is consistent with Old Testament prophecy of the second coming of the lord Jesus Christ.

Zachariah 14:4says

4: And his feet shall stand in that day upon the Mount of Olives, which is before Jerusalem on the east, and the Mount of Olives shall cleave in the midst thereof toward the east and toward the west, and there shall be a very great valley; and half of the mountain shall remove toward the north, and half of it toward the south.

The Scripture above speaks about his second coming. He left from the Mount of Olives in Jerusalem and shall return to the earth through the samemountain.

This second coming is immediately after the Great tribulation which we have already established that it will last for seven years after the Rapture. The lord will ride on a white horse with the armies of heaven riding behind him. The armies of heaven are made up of triumphant saints who were Raptured earlier with Christ. In I Thessalonians 3:13, the Bible says:

13: To the end that he may establish your hearts unblamable in holiness before God, even our father at the coming of our lord Jesus Christ with all his saints.

It clearly shows that the coming of our Lord is with the saints. This is another infallible proof that the post tribulation theory is wrong.

Also in Jude 1:14, the Bible says

14: And Enoch also, the seventh from Adam, prophesied of these, saying, Behold, the Lord cometh with ten thousands of his saints.

Angels are not addressed as saints in the Scriptures. The only 2 sets of people addressed as saints are the Old testaments Saints andthe born againChristians.

BATTLE OFARMAGEDON

He will lead the armies of heaven in a triumphant procession and head straight to capture the Antichrist and the false prophet in Jerusalem and throw them straight into the lake of fire that has been prepared for all unrighteous Souls and the remaining shall he destroy with the sword that proceeds out of His mouth.

Revelations 19:11-16, 19-20 says

11: And I saw heaven opened, and behold a white horse; and He that sat upon him was called Faithful and True, and in righteousness He doth judge and make war.

12: His eyes were as a flame of fire, and on His head were many crowns; and He had a name written, that no man knew, but He Himself.

13: And He was clothed with vesture dipped in blood: and His name is called The Word of God.

14: And the armies which were in heaven followed Him upon white horses, clothed in fine linen, white and clean.

15: And out of his mouth goeth a sharp sword, that with it He should smite the nations: and He shall rule them with a rod of iron: and He treadeth the winepress of the fierceness and wrath of Almighty God.

16: And He hath on his vesture and on his thigh a name written, KING OF KINGS, AND

LORD OFLORDS.

19: And I saw the beast, and the kings of the earth, and their armies, gathered together to make war against him that sat on the horse, and against his army.

20: And the beast was taken, and with him the false prophet that wrought miracles before him, with which he deceived them that had received the mark of the beast, and them that worshipped his image. These both were cast <u>ALIVE</u> into a lake of fire burning with brime stone.

Jesus Christ will order the immediate arrest of Satan. An angel that holds the key of the bottomless pit or the abyss will descend from above and subdue Satan. He will arrest the devil and physically bind him with a very large chain and imprison him in the abyss (tartarus) a place of darkness for a period of one thousand years.

DIFFERENCES BETWEEN THE RAPTURE AND THE SECOND COMING (PAROUSIA)

1. At the Rapture, believers will meet with Christ in the air (I Thessalonians 4:17). While at the second coming, believers will return with the lord to the earth (Revelation 19:14)

2. The Rapture is an event that can happen at any moment

(I Corinthians 15:50, I Thessalonians 5:2) while the second coming will clearly take place at the end of the seven years tribulation (Revelation 6- 19)

3. In the Rapture, believers will be removed from the earth before the earth is judged. (I Thessalonians 5:9) while at the second coming, unbelievers will experience judgment (Matthew 24:40-41).

4. The Rapture will be instant and secret (I Corinthians 15:50-55) while the second coming will be visible to all.

Since the Rapture can take place any moment from now, we as believers must live a life of holiness unto the Lord. Bible says in Hebrews 12:14

14: Follow peace with all men and Holiness, without which no man shall see the Lord.

The mode of the Rapture shows that God will rescue His people prior to His judgment upon the earth because we are not called unto wrath. The situation resembles the pattern of God rescuing Noah and his family in the ark prior to his judgment of the earth by a flood.

One other explanation that supports the pre- tribulation Rapture is the fact that throughout the tribulation period in (Revelation 6-19), the Church was not mentioned, this cannot be an oversight or a coincidence. The most likely explanation is that the Church had already been rescued from the wrath through the event of the Rapture.

MILLENNIUM REIGN

The imprisonment of Satan for one thousand years will usher in the Millennial or Millennium Reign. A millennium is a thousand years. The millennium rule is a one thousand years literal rule of Christ in order to fulfill major Old Testament prophesies.

The headquarters of Christ kingdom will be located at the present Jerusalem and all Jews will return to Israel while the nations will still remain. Example the United States will still remain as United States, Canada will still remain as Canada, Nigeria will still remain Nigeria, Ghana will still remain as Ghana etc.

Isaiah 11:12says

12: And he shall set up an ensign for the nations and shall assemble the outcast of Israel and gather together the disposed of Judah from the four corners of the earth.

Ezekiel 11:17says

17: Therefore say, thus saith the Lord God; I will even gather you from the people, and assemble you out of the countries where you

have been scattered, and I will give you the land ofIsrael.

This period will be the most peaceful period in the history of mankind since the trouble maker and the person that causes the whole of the earth's misfortune would have been imprisoned and Christ absolutely in charge.

At the millennium, Christ, the old time saints and the New Testament saints shall dwell in Jerusalem while the people of the nations especially the righteous who survived the Great tribulation will enter into the millennium in their natural human bodies. Also, some unrighteous relatives of the Antichrist soldiers will also enter the millennium in their natural bodies and will live in the nations. These are the ones that Satan will deceive after the one thousand years millennium rule (Revelation 20:7-10).

Under the rule of Christ, the unrighteous will not be able to challenge Christ, they will conform but not that they are in love with Christ.

Revelation 19:15 says

15: And out of his mouth goeth a sharp sword, that with it he should smite the nations: and he shall rule them with a rod of iron...

This verse clearly shows that the unrighteous people will

be there during the millennium rule, they will be completely submissive to Christ and absolutely helpless and Christ will rule over them with a rod of iron, He wouldn't need a rod of iron to rule Raptured saints who will just be like angels.

The Righteous people in the nations who entered the millennium in their natural human bodies will not need to be ruled by rod of iron. Only the unrighteous will.

The purpose of the millennium rule is to establish Christ as king over all, sitting on the throne of David.

Luke 1:32-33 says

32: He shall be great and shall be called the son of the Highest: and the Lord God shall give unto Him the throne of His father David:

33: And He shall reign over the house of Jacob for ever; and of His kingdom there shall be no end.

These promises will be literally fulfilled by God to Israel. They will bless the other nations (countries), thereby fulfilling the Abrahamic covenant (Genesis 12:1-3).

Israel will take control of the promised geographical borders, there by fulfilling the Palestinian covenant of Deuteronomy 30:1-10. They will also experience forgiveness and a renewed relationship with God, thereby fulfilling the Davidic covenant (2 Samuel 7:10-13)

That millennium kingdom under Christ will give us a taste of what life would have been under Adam and Eve, if they had not sinned. Jesus will be King and Judge (Isaiah 2:4) and we shall reign with him (Revelation 5:10). Animals will live in peace with each other and with humans (Isaiah 11:6-9) and believers will worship God at the new temple. Remember as mentioned earlier, the world will still be divided into nations or countries. Jews will be drawn back into Israel, which will finally have its promised borders (Genesis 17:7-8, Isaiah 11:10-13).

The disciples (Matthew 19:28) and the Raptured saints will rule with Christ over the nations, everybody will live in peace. Although human life shall be prolonged during the millennium as people will live long like trees and there shall be no sickness. There is a misconception that there will be no death during the millennium. Death will continue through the one thousand years for people who violate the laws of Christ. People-both the righteous and the unrighteous who entered the millennium in their natural bodies shall also marry and be given out in marriage and have children.

For those who rebel against Christ, Christ will execute them with the sword from his mouth (Rev 1:16, 2:12 and 19:15). No unrighteousness will be tolerated by Christ.

Isaiah 65:18-25 says

19: I will rejoice over Jerusalem and delight in my people and the sound of weeping and crying will be heard in it no more.

20: No longer will babies die when only a few days old. No longer will adults die before they lived a full life. No longer will people be considered old at one hundred. Only the <u>cursed</u> will <u>DIE</u> that young (NLT).

During this period, the only thing that can lead to death for the unrighteous is rebellion because at that time there shall be NO sickness. Hallelujah! This is also confirmed in the book of Luke 19:27 which says

27: But those mine enemies, which would not that I should reign over them, bring them hither, and slay them before me.

After a thousand years, Satan will be loosened for a short period of time. He will go into the nations to deceive them, note that he will not go to Jerusalem because everybody there is righteous. In a thousand years, the unrighteous will have also multiplied greatly amongst the nations. Though under Christ, they also enjoyed peace but they will not be contented with the strict rule of Christ, so once Satan is released, they will immediately join their master in the last rebellion.

Revelation 20:7-10 says

7: And when the thousand years are expired, Satan shall be loosed out of his prison,

8: And shall go out to deceive the nations which are in the four quarters of the earth, Gog and Magog to gather them together to battle: the number of whom is the same as the sand of the sea.

9: And they went up on the breadth of the earth and compassed the camp of the saints about and the beloved city: and fire came down from God out of heaven and devoured them.

10: And the devil that deceived them was cast into the lake of fire and brimstone, where the beast and the false prophet are, and shall be tormented day and night forever andever.

The above passage describes the final conquest and the end to all rebellion on earth. This battle will not involve Christ, any angel or any saint; it is God against the devil and all his agents. This will be the end of all forms of sin, unrighteousness anddeath.

THE WHITE THRONE JUDGEMENT

Revelation 20:11-15

This is also referred to as the Great white throne Judgment. The judgment seat is before God therefore believers will not appears there. Believers will only appear before the judgment seat of Christ to receive their crowns during the marriage supper of the Lamb. This is confirmed in II

Corinthians 5:10

10: For we must all appear before the judgment seat of Christ; that every one may receive the things done in his body, according to that he hath done, whether it be good or bad.

This is the final judgment of God upon mankind.
After this event, there will be no need for any trial or judgment again….,
God will never need to act as judge again.
Daniel was also given a vision of the great white throne judgment.

Daniel 7:9-10says

9: I beheld till the throne were cast down, and the ancient of days did sit, whose garment was white as snow, and the hair of his head like pure wool: His throne was like the fiery flame and his wheels as burning fire.

10: A fiery stream issued out and came forth from before him: thousands thousands

ministered unto him, and ten thousand times ten thousand stood before him: the judgment was set, and the books were opened.

Whosoever's name was not found written in the book of life will be cast into the lake of fire, hell and death shall also be cast into the lake of fire. This is the second death. Believers in Christ will escape this judgment because their sins have been fully paid by Christ.

Colossians 2:13-14 says

13: And you being dead in your sins and uncircumcision of your flesh, hath He quickened together with Him, having forgiven you all trespasses;

14: Blotting out the hand writing of ordinances that was against us, which was contrary to us, and took it out of the way, nailing it to his cross. Gloryyyyyyyyyyyyy.

CHAPTER TEN

THE NEW HEAVEN,
THE NEW EARTH,
AND THE NEW JERUSALEM

*And I Saw A New Heaven And A New
Earth: For The First Heaven And The
First Earth Were Passed; And There Was
No More Sea*

*And I John Saw The Holy City,
New Jerusalem Coming Down
From God Out Of Heaven,
Prepared*

As A Bride Adorned For Her Husband.

Revelation 21: 1-2

THE NEW HEAVEN,
THE NEW EARTH AND
THE NEW JERUSALEM

In Revelation 21:5, Bible says

5: And He that sat upon the throne said beholds I make all things new. And He said unto me, write: for these words are true and faithful.

Immediately after the final battle against the final rebellion, the amount of destruction will require reconstructing all things. Moreover, the current heaven, earth and the present Jerusalem have been corrupted by ungodly presence of Satan and his demons and unrighteous people.

II Peter 3:10, 13 says

10: but the day of the Lord will come as a thief in the night; in the which the heavens shall pass away with great noise, and the elements shall melt with fervent heat, the earth also and the works that are therein shall be burned up.

13: Nevertheless we, according to his promise look for new heavens, a new earth, therein dwellethrighteousness.

A NEWHEAVEN

God will create a new heaven. The throne of God is

in heaven and will remain in heaven. The Scripture says heaven belongs to God and the earth has He given to the children of men. Heaven is not to be permanently inhabited by men. Before the advent of Christ, when righteous men die, they go to the same place with the unrighteous but different compartments separated by a wide gulf which cannot be crossed by any of the parties from one side to the other. One compartment is paradise while the other compartment for the unrighteous is hell and all are taken captive there by Satan.

Luke 16:20-26 says

20: And there was a certain beggar named Lazarus, which was laid at his gate, full of sores,

21: And desiring to be fed with the crumbs which fell from the rich man's table: moreover, the dogs came and licked his sores.

22: And it came to pass that the beggar died and was carried by the angels into Abraham's bosom: the rich man also died and wasburied;

23: and in hell he lifted up his eyes, being in torment and seeth Abraham afar off and Lazarus in his bosom.

24: And he cried and said, father Abraham have mercy on me and send

Lazarus, that he may dip the tip of his finger in water and cool my tongue; for I am tormented in this flame.

25 But Abraham said, son, remember that thou in thy life time receivedst thy good things, and likewise Lazarus evil things: but now he is comforted and thou art tormented.

26: And beside all this, between us and you there is a great gulf fixed: so that they which would   pass from hence to   you cannot; neither can they pass to us, that would come from thence.

Can you see that they could even see themselves.

When Christ died, he liberated the righteous from the grip of Satan and lifted paradise into heaven (**Matthew 27:50-53, Revelation 1:17-18**). In **Ephesians 4:8-10**, the Bible says he went into the lower parts of the earth and took captivity (Satan) captive.

On the way to heaven with the triumphant saints, some saints who were liberated from the shackles of Satan made appearance to their people in the holy city.

Matthew 27:52-53 *says*

52: And the graves were opened; and many bodies of the saints which slept arose,

53: And came out of the graves after His resurrection, and went into the holy city, and appeared unto many.

Today, when a believer dies, he/she goes to heaven, awaiting his/her final destination which is the New Jerusalem while the unbeliever goes to hell preparing for his/her final destination which is the lake of fire. Remember, hell and death shall be cast into the lake of fire which is the second death. Heaven belongs to God eternally.

THE NEW EARTH

God will create the new earth which will also warehouse the New Jerusalem, but the two places are two distinct places.

Remember that in the last chapter we spoke about the nations. God will still divide the new earth into nations. Is this surprising? Remember that some people will enter into the millennium in their natural human bodies. They will eventually be given a glorified body which cannot die again after the millennium. They will live in different nations as kingdoms and carry out the plan that God initiated through Adam. They will marry and bear children and replenish the earth and subdue it. There shall be no more sickness or sin.

Remember the Bible says that the gate of the New Jerusalem shall not be shut day or night and the kings of the nation shall bring their glory into it.

Revelation 21: 24-26 says

24: And the nation of them which are saved shall walk in the light of it and the kings of the earth do bring their glory into it.

25: And the gates of it shall not be shut at all by day: for there shall be no night there.

26: And they (people of the new earth) shall bring the glory and honor of the nation into it.

(Emphasis is mine). Read also Revelation. *22:2*

Please note that the Scriptures above where the nations are mentioned are event after the millennium. So the new earth will be exactly like the time of Adam and eve before the fall of man.

THE NEW JERUSALEM

The New Jerusalem is the final destination of the old time saints and the New Testament saints.
At that time, we will be like angels that cannot marry and cannot be given out in marriage (Mark 12:25). We will be with Christ in that beautiful city.

The city is a master piece; it is a beautiful work of a skilled craftsman. This is described in details in Revelation 21:9-27.

The city will come down from the new heaven from God the master architect (Revelation 21:10). It will have the glory of GOD, its radiance like a most rare jewel, like a japer, clear as crystal (Revelation 21:11)

The city has a great high wall with twelve gates and twelve angels at the gates with the name of the twelve tribes of Israel inscribed on each gate. Three gates at each of the north, south, east, and west gates sides. It is built on twelve foundation each having the names of the apostles of our Lord Jesus Christ (Revelation 21:12-14)

The city is a cube, same length, width and height. It is four square. The length is about one thousand five hundred miles and a total surface area of thirteen million five hundred thousand square miles. There will be buildings into the sky which extends one thousand five hundred miles into the sky.

Its walls are built of jasper while the city is pure gold, like clear glass. The foundation is adorned by all manner of precious stones. The twelve gates are twelve pearls and the street is pure gold.

The city does not need the sun or the moon because the Lord Almighty and the Lamb are the lights of it. Neither does it have a temple because the Almighty God and the Lord Jesus Christ are the temple thereof. There we will worship God day without night forever and ever. Amen. There shall be no sorrow or curses there because God shall make all

things new. He will wipe away all tears.
Revelation 21:4 *says*

> **4: And God shall wipe away all tears from their eyes; and there shall be no more death, neither sorrow, nor crying, neither shall there be any more pain: for the former things are passed away.**

Apostle John didn't have sufficient words to describe the city; the beauty of the city is beyond imagination and description. Imagine a city that is built by a perfect God, the Master builder, the Greatest designer, the Greatest architect, the Greatest craftsman.

May I never miss this city in Jesus Christ mighty name (Amen).

I pray for you also that you will not miss this city in Jesus Christ mighty name (Amen)

I trust God that you are blessed by this work.

I started writing this book on 16th April 2020 and completed it on the 24th April, 2020 at: 17:15PM,

To God's Glory, this is one of the benefits of the Corona virus lockdown!

THANK YOU JESUS!

ABOUT THE AUTHOR

Adeyinka Adebisi Lawani is the senior Pastor of the Beauty of Christ Ministry, an end time Ministry devoted to teaching the undiluted Word of God with unction especially Eschatology (end time based events) and reaching out to lost souls.

He served as a Minister and Pastor for Twenty Five years in the Redeemed Christian Church of God. He retired as a management staff in the Banking industry. He holds a Bachelor's degree in Operations Research from Federal University of Technology Yola and MBA (Finance) from University of Ilorin with about seventeen years banking experience.

He is married to Oluwakemi Olushola Lawani an evangelist. They are blessed with four boys, they reside in Lagos Nigeria where they run the ministry together.